Thank you for buying the second edition of the Football and Real Ale Guide,

I have improved this guide thanks to the comments of the readers of last year's guides.

Pub selection criteria

The pubs are selected if they have been recommended to me as:-

- Friendly to visiting away fans
- Have a good selection of well kept real ale.
- Are located close, but not too close to the ground
- In each town I tried to get a balance of large, small, good food and community based pubs
- I have visited every pub and talked to those in charge

The maps

The new maps locate the pubs and the grounds. They were compiled under licence by Dotted Eyes of Bromsgrove.

The pub descriptions

The beer list is now organised in alphabetical order of the brewer and then beer. Ciders are given if they are on draught, after the beers.

The new food descriptions are direct quotations from the landlord. I do not sample food but take the advice of the locals as to the best pub to combine the beer with a meal.

I also now give pub opening times. They give closing times but, as with all pubs, they have freedom to extend the hours beyond those given here.

Taxis

I have included a list of taxis numbers in the guide. They are not recommendations but are often ones that I used over the year.

The Photographs

All photographs were taken by myself and on the day of my visit except where I visited late in the evening and had to return the next morning.

Awards

Throughout the guide you will find pages that indicate that some pubs are deserving of extra recognition. The divisional awards were voted for by readers and those I

met ...
cho ...
ent ...
mo ...

Le...

The league tables of last year certainly created some comment over the year and especially so in the towns that were near the bottom of the league. They are included again by popular demand and are slightly more sophisticated because I have tried to balance the number of ales in the pubs with the number of alternatives in the town.

Cultural Guides

I am really pleased that Glyn accepted my offer to write for the guides. When you read the pages please do so in the spirit in which they were written. How often have you thought about going to an away game only to think that there will be time to fill before opening, people and friends to consider or, what else can I find to justify the trip? How often late in the evening have you found yourself looking for something to say about a place that you have visited and wanted something more to say than 'The beer was good'? Glyn might just give you some excuses/topics of conversation/trivia that could get you a pass out the next time you wish to visit.

Some comments may offend. In this case they are all Glyn's and writs should be sent to him. At other times you will be amused and then congratulatory notes can be sent to me. At all times the guides offer an alternative look at British cities by someone who describes himself as 'permanently angry with things that don't really matter.' Unfortunately, however, some of the comments do matter and without people getting angry in a typically British way then much of what we love in the urban landscape will be lost. Should you ever meet Glyn I do offer some advice. Don't get into a conversation about Pylons. Life is just too short.

The Website

The website offers the best place to order, buy and comment on the pubs.

www.footballandrealaleguide.co.uk

Stedders June 2006

I never visit a place before reviewing it, it prejudices a man so.
Adapted from a quote by Sydney Smith (1771-1845)

I wrote the first Bradwan Cultural Guide for the City Gent in 2001 and about half the Guides here are rewrites of Gent articles, so there are variations in style. I did not write them to please an imaginary audience, but to share my enthusiasms and occasionally my anger. From an early age I visited places because I was curious about everything. When I started drinking beer and travelling to away games I continued to explore the towns I was drinking and watching in. I have no problem fitting real ale, football and culture together in my head, and hope what I have written will be of some interest to most, and raise a smile and some enthusiasm in at least a few.

I believe there are good and dreadful ways to run most things including football clubs and towns. Websites that freeze my computer or have no links for visitors are annoying: and getting lost when sober because there are no maps, signposts or street names suggests a badly managed place; especially where millions have been spent on nagging notices. People warm to friendly welcomes, but are less likely to return if they are abused, or treated like savages or idiots.

The Guides are around 250 words, which limited the web links and information I could include. Please check everything for yourself. If you end up outside a locked and rain soaked attraction with a complaining significant other and grizzling parental responsibilities it's your fault.

One author found particularly useful was Simon Inglis. His *The Football Grounds of Great Britain* was the first and best of its kind, and his latest, *Engineering Archie*, provided much historical background, especially for London. Glyn Watkins' dubious biography

Like Richard Stedman I support a struggling football club, drink proper beer, did time in teaching, and am a publisher. Unlike him I sometimes cook, can go days without visiting the pub, draw, write poetry and occasionally get angry. I created my first book *Walburgas forgetting – forgiving* when pneumonia stopped me supply teaching, and left me too ill for anything physical but not ill enough to sleep all day. To stop me going mad, or madder, I made a book of some drawings and poems I had done over 20 years. When I got better I made and sold about a hundred more. After being awarded a business start up grant I published them, and organised a launch at the *National Museum of Photography, Film & Television.* This involved me finding the last remaining print of a film called *A Month in the Country*, based on a book by JL Carr and starring Colin Firth, Natasha Richardson and Kenneth Branagh. I also persuaded Channel 4 to release it on DVD for the first time.

I produced my second book, *The Wayne Jacobs Little Red Head Book – A Red Headed Footballer & the Mysteries of Red Hair* because Wayne Jacobs is a decent bloke and footballer whose testimonial year was seemingly being forgotten because Bradford City being in administration, again. I sold hundreds and gave over £200 to Wayne's testimonial fund. I have also done other handmade books, including *Highway to ULL. Hayseed Dixie, hillbilly rock, highlands, alcohol, Finland & fish*, when I was Poet in Residence at the first Loopallu festival in Ullapool.

I have done a few other things, including creating a JB Priestley Night, which involved piping in a meat and potato pie with a cornet playing On Ilkley Moor Baht'at. I am presently working on a documentary script and connected book entitled: Lines of Power – Lines of Pleasure. The history and poetry of pylons.

Visit *www.bradwan.com* for more about me and to buy my books

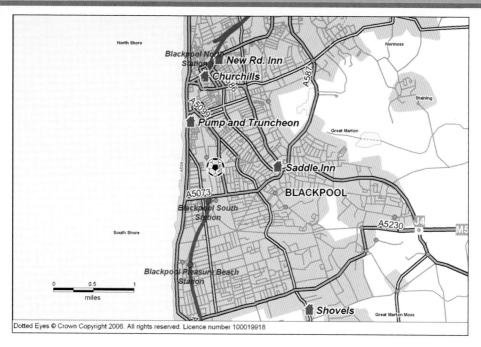

Dotted Eyes © Crown Copyright 2006. All rights reserved. Licence number 100019918

Churchills

83-85 Topping Street, FY1 3AY. Telephone 01353 662026 204955 **New**
Gaffer: John Slowik
Smoking Throughout
Food: Good pub grub from 12
Open: 10.30 to 11 Mon to Thu, 10.30 to 12 Fri and Sat, 12 to 12 Sun

The Churchill Inn is relatively easy to find. Head for the Winter Gardens and then walk away from the crowds towards the station. A group of discerning locals will have beaten you to it but the pub will stand out as looking like a proper pub on a typically English town street corner.,

MP | BM | PG

The locals come in all shapes and sizes so it was with some ease that I fitted into the smaller front snug for a quiet pint and a bit of welcome relief from Blackpool's daytime stresses. It is then that you notice that the entertainment does exist here. This evening was to be psychic night, and another time finds Mr Blackpool doing whatever Mr Blackpool does. A chat with John, the landlord, enlightened me as to the family nature of the entertainment and the fact that footie fans have a diversion that involves staying here when their team is in a particularly poor run of form.

The beer quality was good, in this case national choices following me up the M6 from the South and East. The locals were very friendly, – even an offer of good cheap accommodation at the nearby Darfield Hotel was mentioned by one of the regulars. All in all, the pub is a great find, one that restores your faith in the real town of Blackpool.

BWV 10.10.05: Bateman *XXXB*, Greene King *Old Speckled Hen, Ruddles County*, Wells *Bombardier*

New Road Inn

244 Talbot Road, FY1 3HL. Telephone 01253 62887 2370429
Gaffer: Mark Penistone
Separate smoking areas
Open: 10.30 to 12

The New Road Inn is also conveniently located, being 100 m from the North station, opposite the Mecca. As it is a regular CAMRA award winner you should guess that the ale is good and the range greater at the weekends than shown here.

Mark is proud to designate it as a no-nonsense drinkers' pub. He sells himself short here because it offers more than spit and sawdust, along with its no-nonsense approach to '*the fools who expect something different to what we are*'. Bring your mates for a really friendly welcome. Bring your girlfriend who might well enjoy the security of such a safe pub. The ownership has recently transferred to W+D but the policy for good ale remains and the choice often includes a mild. The latest development is to offer ciders and a perry. The non - smoking section lies to the rear in what is sometimes a private meeting room. The other great feature of this snug was the fantastic photographic exhibition in place during my visit. The art changes on a monthly basis, showcasing local artists. Some may also be interested in wireless internet access being available, although Barney the Dog represents what most want to see in such a pub rather than the weary pub reviewer typing up these notes. With a warning to '*watch your nuts*', I left to roam the streets of the North Shore. The minimalist chic of the New Road certainly made an impression, as did the warmth of the welcome.

BWV 10.10.05: Jennings *Bitter, Cumberland Ale, Snecklifter*, Titanic *White Star*, Weston's *Herefordshire Perry, Old Rosie Cider*

Pump and Truncheon

Bonny Street, FY1 5AR Telephone 01253 751176
www.pumpandtruncheon.co.uk
Gaffer: Keith Slater
Food: Hot and cold home cooked food from 12
Smoking Throughout
Open: 10.30 to 11 Mon to Thu, 10.30 to 12 Fri and Sat, 12 to 12 Sun

This pub has a '*boys in blue*' theme and a hint of cell life in its décor. Friendly staff and a regular mix of ale fans and those eating food make this a popular and convenient place. Complete with casks to stand around they also stage '*entertainment*'. Perhaps this is a fine choice for a traditional weekend in the town; it stays open later than most and is just behind the seafront arcades and '*fun*.' This has been a long time favourite of mine and it's good to see the good elements remain unaltered as all around it go for the quick buck. The locals are particularly used to seeing tourists and away fans finding it for only one time a year. On those rare hot summers days the pub is a very oasis in the sometimes noisy and sticky streets. The beer choice is always innovative and is good enough to guarantee a wide range of drinkers will seek it out. This pub has won numerous real ale awards, as it should.

UPDATE: The pub has changed little, still good beer and fun to drink in. Boddingtons Bitter is the regular ale and four others continue to rotate.

BWV 23.11.04: Archers *Goodwill*, Blackpool *BPA*, Boddingtons *Cask Bitter*, Copper Dragon *Golden Ale*, Ridley's *Rumpus*
BWV 10.10.05: Archers *Delivery*, Boddingtons *Bitter*, Castle Rock *Elsie Mo*, Phoenix *White Monk*, Slaters *Supreme*

Saddle Inn

286 Whitegate Drive, FY3 9PH. Telephone 01253 607921
Gaffer: Alan Bedford
Food: Good value fresh menu with good portions 12 to 2, 5 to 7 Mon to Fri,
12 to 3 Sat, 1 to 4 Sun
Separate smoking areas
Opening Times: 12 to 11, 12 to 10.30 Sun

This is a very old roadside inn with three excellent rooms around a traditional bar. The bar itself is worthy of mention because of its design that leaves anyone tall, like me, bending down to get a view of the bar staff serving you. Each room is very comfortable, retaining elements of the original room structure, separate rooms rather than modern-style drinking areas. My weekday visit found a great mix of luncheoners, locals and real ale tickers. I recommend the room with sporting photos that tell stories of a rich local heritage. Here the locals talk of glories past, of massive crowds at Bloomfield Road and of the hopes for future successes as the ground is redeveloped.
UPDATE: Landlord Alan Bedford has taken over the pub and plans real ale festivals. *'It is my passion'* Norman, remains the oldest swinger in the pub and, as Nora said, it really is *'a second home to friends in town.'*

BWV 23.11.04: Marston's *Pedigree*, Orkney *Dark Island*, Woodforde's *Wherry*
BWV 10.10.05: Adnams *Bitter*, Bass *Draught*, Butcombe *Bitter*, Harviestoun *Ptarmigan*, Moorhouses *Pendle Witches Brew*

The Shovels

260 Commonedge Road, Malton, FY4 5DH. Telephone 01253 762702
Gaffer: Steve Norris
Food: Extensive family pub menu 12 to 9.30 daily
Separate smoking areas
Opening Times: 11 to 11, 12 to 10.30 Sun

Here we have a new farmhouse style pub with a footie and real ale fanatic landlord to boot. This is the place to indulge yourself. Steve will know your favourite ale houses from personal experience and offers a challenge that says a beer you haven't tried before will always be on offer. Try it especially if you fancy a weekend real ale extravaganza. Steve encourages groups who can phone in advance for a tailor-made visit. It is often also used by those visiting Preston who want to mix and match their ale and amusements. Can you name another pub with three non-league football grounds within 100 yards? I would also recommend picking up the local CAMRA guide where Steve often writes of his footie-related real ale trips following his Mackem dream. Large and also local, this is more than just an estate gastro-pub. It puts the ale to the forefront of its marketing and is rightly very popular.
UPDATE: Beer festival (80 beers) in late October.

BWV 23.11.04: Goff's *Camelot*, Hart *Chinook*, Tom Wood *Jolly Ploughman*, Oakham *JHB*, Wychwood *Three Wyches*
BWV 10.10.05: Anglo Dutch *Spike's on T'Way*, Boddingtons *Bitter*, Foxfield *Tigertops*, *Waterside*, Hart *Ice Maiden*, Theakston's *Best*

Blackpool

Blackpool is unsophisticated and unpretentious so you either love it or you hate it. It may be Chavpool-by-the-Sea but millions have been spending money here for nearly two centuries, so it is doing something right.

The Beach

Blackpool beach is big and now it's clean. The days are long gone when you could flush the toilet on the promenade, run down to the sewage outlet and watch your contribution to bio-mass float off into the Irish Sea.

Dr Who Exhibition and Museum

This is Blackpool's second Dr Who museum, the Patrick Troughton version if you like. Dr Who started in 1963, when the BBC were producing well written, enjoyable family entertainment (seeing that today would require a working Tardis). It scared children enough for many to watch it from behind the armchair; Do children do that anymore, unless they are breaking and entering? This museum costs six Quid. Without a profit any private museum will be exterminated, like the first museum and the Laurel and Hardy museum that used to be here as well. *www.drwhoexhibitions.co.uk*

Stanley Park

Parks and libraries are two of the finest Victorian contributions to civic culture, marks of pride, purpose and self improvement. Now our libraries are being exterminated by tax eating Daleks who hate books. Parks are harder to kill, and a well kept park is still a credit to a town, and Stanley Park is one of the best.

The Grundy Art Gallery

A very good gallery, with natural lighting, the collection includes Paul Nash, one of Bradwan's favourites. *www.aboutbritain.com/GrundyArtGallery*

Bournemouth

Two centuries ago Bournemouth was a sandy heath cut by steep sided 'chines' with the Bourne running at the bottom of the biggest. It became a fashionable resort for people suffering chest problems, with pines being planted to scent the air as an aid to breathing. The railway came late to Bournemouth, possibly because the people living here didn't want the unwashed masses visiting, spending pennies, and driving away the Guinea spending nobs. The nobs started holidaying abroad anyway, but Bournemouth remained a posh place. The 'sea front' holiday part feels like a different town to the part where senior social workers and other glories of their class live.

Boscombe

Dean Court is in Boscombe, a few miles east of the mouth of the Bourne. You can walk there along the sea front, passing Britain's second public nudist beach. The first was at Brighton, on a beach of pebbles and pain. Bournemouth's is sandy, so if you want to run naked into the sea you wont have to worry about walking on pebbles, just about them dropping off because of the cold if you visit in winter.

Bournemouth seems to have lost three museums: the Rothesay Museum, the Big Four Railway Museum and the Typewriter Museum have gone to the great museum in the sky; or land fill in the ground: leaving the Russell-Cotes Art Gallery & Museum. We are sorry that there is no longer a British typewriter museum. Invented in 1868, extinct within 130 years, and now almost forgotten.

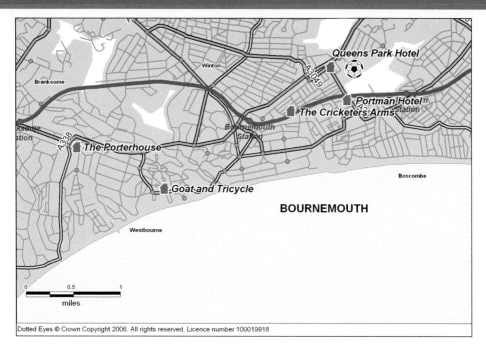

Dotted Eyes © Crown Copyright 2006. All rights reserved. Licence number 100019918

The Cricketers Arms

New

41 Windham Road, BH1 4RN. Telephone 01202 551589
Gaffer: Sheila Doherty
Food: Sunday roasts only 12 to 4
Smoking Throughout
Open: 11 to 11 Mon to Thu, 12 to 12 Fri and Sat, 12 to 10.30 Sun

| CP | SKY | JB | PG | D |

The '*Cricks*' is one of those pubs that should be really famous yet has managed to keep some anonymity that I am reluctant to blow. It is a back-street boozer that has some very curious features and attitudes. From the outside it suggests nothing extra-ordinary and then you enter to four great separate bars all with something special. The main bar or '*private bar*' is where I found the locals in full flow, engaging in banter with Sheila and very funny it was too. The star attraction is the lounge; apparently this vaulted stable was once the boxing gym for none other than Freddie Mills. Then there are the posters that will keep many an aged rocker engrossed.

The beer rotates regularly and was truly excellent. You might find a quiet space as there are numerous nooks and crannies. To do so, however, would be to miss out on the craic. Shelia is a marvellous host, a true friend it seems to her regulars as well as the new venturers who do discover that the 15 min. walk to the ground is easy, so too the stroll to the station.

And then to add to the quirkiness I was introduced to President Bush. He was about to lose his space in the toy collection to a Ninja Turtle. Well what could be more appropriate? I had at last found a good back-street boozer in Bournemouth and one contented beer hunter found it very hard to leave for the cold early evening air.

BWV 6.1.06: Fuller's *London Pride*, Hardys and Hanson *Rocking Rudolph*, Titanic *White Star*

Goat and Tricycle

27-29 West Hill Road, BH2 5PF. Telephone 01202 314220
Gaffers: James and Trish Blake
Food: freshly prepared homemade food to order 12 to 2, 6 to 9 Mon to Thu 6 to 8.30 Fri
Separate smoking areas
Open: 12 to 3, 5 to 11 Mon to Thu, 12 to 11.30 Fri and Sat 12 to 3, 7 to 11 Sun

SP **TV** **BM** **D**

This is a split-level pub that adds an impressive quality range of local brews. Locals recommend '*the courtyard, all hanging baskets and sunshine.*' Others suggest '*it is the only real ale pub left in town*' (Lindsay of Bournemouth), '*a relief from the disco pubs taking over the town.*' They go on to comment that '*it is the closest pub to the ground (2 miles or so).*' It is very handy to local hotels, yet close enough to the town centre for other entertainment. I would not travel far from here as the atmosphere was very relaxed, comfortable and the choice of ale very tempting. You can see why it '*was East Dorset Pub of the Year having friendly helpful staff*' (Gemma.) I was assured the food was indeed freshly prepared and therefore, we now have a top quality real ale pub in a rather beer-bereft town centre.
UPDATE: There are plans for a refit in the next year. Further awards include Meridian area cask real ale Pub of the year. The conference room and gallery may become more of a feature.

BWV 6.1.06: Exmoor *Fox*, Greene King *Abbot*, *Fireside*, *Badger Festive Pheasant*, Theakston's *Best*, Wadworth *6X*, *The Bishop's Tipple*, *Henry's IPA*, *JCB*
BWV 9.2.05: Arundel *Wet Willie*, Caledonian *80/-*, Fuller's *ESB*, Greene King *1799*, Highgate *Old Ale*, Ringwood *Fortyniner*, Wadworth *6X*, *IPA*, *JCB*, Wychwood *Dirty Tackle*, Wyre Piddle *Piddle in the Dark*

The Porterhouse

113 Poole Road, Westbourne BH4 9BG. Telephone 01202 768586   **New**
Gaffer: Jonathon Blackie
Food: Rolls and sandwiches all day
Smoking Throughout
Open: 11 to 11. 12 to 10.30 Sun

MP **PG**

I was really hoping to find a town-centre ale house this year but every time I talked to the locals they kept on directing me to the Porterhouse. Westbourne, a suburban village is accessible by the M1/M2 buses and many of the yellow buses so I was rewarded by a great early morning beer in this quality Ringwood ale house.

I arrived the week before new managers arrived so things might change but I doubt the locals will let that happen. The single bar is a wooden floor adult games room. Reading material lines the walls, as do board games. By 11.45 the first crib games were starting and space at the bar was limited to locals. The talk was relaxed and the welcome very helpful. Indeed the final recommendation came directly from one such good old boy. I hid my nose in the Sudoku as others glimpsed page three of the Guardian. The pub was spotless, highly cherished and perfectly local to the High Street. A mobile went off despite the poster that discouraging its use. Chatting to Alice and her bloke, I gathered that the footie routine involved locals going to nearby big screens and returning afterwards for a real ale session. Other regular visitors are those who attend conferences and have a CAMRA member in their number. The Porterhouse is a great local, well worth combining with a visit to the Goat.

BWV 6.1.06: Kelham Island *Pale Rider*, Ringwood *Best*, *Fortyniner*, *Old Thumper*, *Porter*, Thatcher's' *Farmers Tipple Cider*

Portman Hotel

Ashley Road, BH1 4LT. Telephone 01202 393499
www.portmanhotel.com
Gaffer: Mike Lee
F Excellent home cooked fresh food, daily specials with restaurant next door
12 to 10 Mon to Sat, 12 to 9 Sun
Smoking Throughout
Open: 11 to 11, 12 to 11 Sun

Just when all was lost trawling the streets of Bournemouth for ale any real ale, I stumbled upon a form of beer and music heaven. This pub has it all, and most importantly, top quality ale and a real buzz. My visit included a free listen to the jamming session next door, that's what I call background music. It has been modernized within its original shell and more is to come. One day the top class restaurant attracts serious foodies while on Saturday the menu transforms to be footie friendly. You get *'Lots of extras here, like steak for a fiver on Saturdays, live music in the Green Room on weekends and the Soul to Soul restaurant which is definitely not pub grub.'* A great pub and one to watch as it becomes even more popular.' The popularity of the Portman will inevitably increase over the next few years, especially as the outside appearance is improved to entice the more prejudiced street pub crawler to come inside.
UPDATE: The refurbishment will include good value and good quality accommodation. (From £20) Changes to the music include regular cabaret nights. Can you feel a weekend away coming up? Give Mike a call.

BWV 6.1.06: Fuller's *London Pride*, Isle of Purbeck *IPA*, Ringwood *Best*
BWV 9.2.05: Greene King *IPA*. Ringwood *Bitter*, Wadworth *6X*

Queens Hotel

482 Holdenhurst Road, BH9 8AR. Telephone 01202 720096
Gaffers: Alan and Chris Newton
Food: Everything from rolls to steaks from 10 but just rolls on match days
Smoking Throughout
Open: 10 to 12, 10 to 1am Fri to Sat, 12 to 12 Sun

This is the *'world famous'* Queens Park, made famous by recommendations to this guide but also in the flag seen throughout the Barmy Army globe. *'No longer a hotel, it is very friendly place.'* This is a pub in the old style. Catering for traditional pub users it has large rooms set aside for pub games, food, chatting and watching Sky TV. While real ale isn't the raison d'etre, the beer on offer was surprisingly good for a pub so close to the ground. This place is always crowded on matchdays and people often spill into the back courtyard and car park. My visit coincided with an England international friendly match on the TV, boring match, yet great entertainment as locals came in and later left wishing they had arrived earlier than the game had started. I left them to their supping and made a promise to come back on a matchday, to relive the good lunchtime sessions held here in the past. Only two minutes from the ground and is really the only pub within five minutes of the stadium. Home supporters often use the club bars.
UPDATE: Apart from extending opening hours, nothing has changed much other than away fans being directed to the left hand bar, home to the right.

BWV 9.2.05: Ringwood *Bitter*
BWV 6.1.06: Ringwood *Bitter*

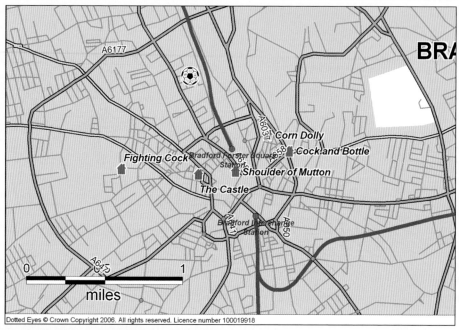

Dotted Eyes © Crown Copyright 2006. All rights reserved. Licence number 100019918

The Castle

New

20 Grattan Road, BD1 2LU. Telephone 01274 393166
Gaffer: Paul Chand
Food: Sandwiches
Smoking Throughout
Open: 11 to 11, 12 to 10.30 Sun

SP SKY BM PG D

The Castle is a truly impressive building. The stone-faced Yorkshire edifice hides a real local that has a grand scale in its interior layout. It was closed for refurbishment and rescue when I toured Bradford in 2005 and there was much concern as to its future. Therefore, it was great to receive a call from Paul asking whether I might visit this year as he wanted to re-establish the Castle as a popular venue on the town real ale scene. Paul has done a great job and the plans for the future are truly exciting. This included a real ale policy that always has a dark beer, nationals and rarer local ales as shown below. This large street-corner pub lies just out of the town centre but convenient for those making the pilgrimage to the Fighting Cock. Developments have included a totally new cellar and over the next year the pub will undergo massive improvements on the décor that will build on the traditional style of the pub. A tap room and beer festivals will also be other great developments in the coming year.

You can only be grabbed by Paul's enthusiasm. Paul No. 2 runs the bar and is a perfect gent, talking of real ale and pub life with genuine love and affection. Talk to Paul and his love of music suggests that this will also feature heavily in the news that the pub will inevitably create. It is already a good pub that will soon be very very good.

BWV 1.3.06: Jennings *Cockerhoop*, Mansfield *Cask Ale*, Marston's *Pedigree*, Mordue *Black Midden Stout*, Red Brick *Double Barrel*

Cock and Bottle

93 Barkerend Road, BD3 9AA. Telephone 01274 222305
www.williamgreenwood.com
Gaffer: Peter Fell
Food: All home-cooked traditional style pub grub 12 to 2.30
Separate smoking areas
Open: 11.30 to 12, 11.30 to 1 Fri to Sun

The recent history of this street-corner pub is fascinating and deserves full documentation, alas elsewhere. It is the future that excites this writer because, having being reopened as the tap for the William Greenwood Brewery, it surely

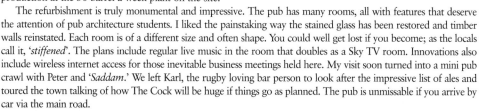

will be a destination for real ale lovers visiting the town. I met with Peter and friends on the day they finally started production at the 50 barrel a week plant on the site.

The refurbishment is truly monumental and impressive. The pub has many rooms, all with features that deserve the attention of pub architecture students. I liked the painstaking way the stained glass has been restored and timber walls reinstated. Each room is of a different size and often shape. You could well get lost if you become; as the locals call it, '*stiffened*'. The plans include regular live music in the room that doubles as a Sky TV room. Innovations also include wireless internet access for those inevitable business meetings held here. My visit soon turned into a mini pub crawl with Peter and '*Saddam.*' We left Karl, the rugby loving bar person to look after the impressive list of ales and toured the town talking of how The Cock will be huge if things go as planned. The pub is unmissable if you arrive by car via the main road.

BWV 1.3.06: Black Sheep *Riggwelter*, Dent *Bitter*, Kelham Island *Pale Rider*, Marston's *Pedigree*, Oakham *Kaleidascope*, Rudgate *Well Blathered*, Timothy Taylor *Landlord*, Wensleydale *Forresters Bitter*, William Greenwood *Fat Prop, Flying Winger*

Corn Dolly

110 Bolton Road, BD1 4DE. Telephone 01274 720219
Gaffer: Neil Dunkin
Food: Good honest pub grub 12 to 2 Mon to Fri, Sandwiches match days
Smoking Throughout
Open: 11.30 to 11, 12 to 10.30 Sun

The Corn Dolly is a single bar, timber and plaster framed, that serves really good and rarer ales to add to the national standards. Bradford CAMRA awards stand proud in the pub as does a fascinating painting of Bradford legend Ces Podd. Add in a pool table and you get the feeling that this is a proper community pub that has welcomed beer hunting guests into their midst. I enjoyed a brief lunchtime visit and soon felt that I had found a much - loved refuge just outside the town centre. The food comes recommended so it is therefore my city centre choice, perhaps the pub to visit after the game if you are aiming to get a later train home. I had a great chat with Neil and his returning friend, gleaning valuable insights into the other city centre ale houses.
UPDATE: Three different visits this year, all were excellent. Neil was often on holiday!

BWV 14.3.05: Black Sheep *Bitter*, Cottage *Merchant Navy*, Durham *White Gold*, Everards *Tiger*, Glentworth *Bad March*, Hopback *Summer Lightning*, Moorhouses *Dolly Bitter*, Timothy Taylor *Landlord*
BWV1.3.06: Anglo Dutch *Spike's On T'Way*, Black Sheep *Bitter*, Bowland *Double Centurion*, Durham *Bishop's Gold*, Everards *Tiger*, Holden's *Black Country Special*, Moorhouses *Dolly Bitter*, Timothy Taylor *Landlord*

Fighting Cock

21-23 Preston Street, BD7 1JE. Telephone 01274 726907
Gaffer: Sue Turner
Food: Good value home-cooked hot and cold lunches 12 to 4 Not Sun
Smoking Throughout SP TV JB
Open: 11 to 11, 12 to 10.30 Sun

The Cock is an award-winning boozer that would be popular in any town or location. In Bradford it sits isolated in an industrial estate, yet still draws the devoted from afar. The pull is more than a predictable beer followed by a curry, rather then joy of finding great beer in a tap room atmosphere to die for. It looks, and indeed smells, like a serious pub. One can imagine rough cut cigarettes and talk of the good old days among the regulars who are far too young to know what they were. I would always make an effort to get to this pub. The locals comment on the great juke box.

UPDATE: Just as brilliant, Local CAMRA awards: Pub of the Year 2005, Winter Season 2005

BWV 14.3.05: Bank Top *Port O'Call*, Glentworth *Early Spring*, Greene King *Abbot*, Holden's *Thigh Bones*, Kelburn *Goldihops*, Old Mill *Bitter*, Phoenix *White Monk*, Theakston's *Old Peculier*, Timothy Taylor *Golden Best*, *Landlord*, Biddenden's *Dry Cider*, Monk's *Delight Cider*, Weston's *Old Rosie*
BWV.1.3.06: Bradfield *Blonde*, Castle Rock *Hemlock*, Copper Dragon *Golden Pippin*, Goose Eye *Golden Eye*, Greene King *Abbot*, Old Mill *Bitter*, Phoenix *White Monk*, Pictish *Brewers Gold*, Theakston's *Old Peculier*, Timothy Taylor *Best*, *Golden Best*, *Landlord*, Biddenden *Dry*, *Monk's Delight Cider*, Weston's *Old Rosie*

Shoulder of Mutton **New**

28 Kirkgate, BD1 1QL. Telephone 01274 726038
Gaffer: Paul Cokey
Food: All home cooked Yorkshire/English menu 12 to 2.30 Not Sun
No smoking at bar
Open: 11 to 11 Mon to Sat, 12 to 10.30 Sun

The second port of call for Peter, DJ Deaf and myself was this beautiful and somewhat relaxing town centre pub. It had also come highly recommended by the crew at the *City Gent*, so I was very happy to set into the OBB at a price that all find remarkable. This is a truly friendly and intimate town centre pub that instantly invites cross-table conversation as I found when the group was extended to some regulars enjoying and praising the merits of '*their*' local.

The pub has many small rooms and a fantastic pub courtyard. The impressiveness comes from the towering walls of the surrounding buildings and the fact it is cool in summer and wind-free in winter. I wondered how this pub is not '*listed*.' It oozes character that is enhanced by having no music, games or machines. Chris and Annie introduced me to Billy, Arif and friends; it is just that type of pub. It is so easy to get into easy chat. The pub is not on the main town drag and will be quieter than the usual town centre pub on matchdays, which would suit me just fine. It is a good honest boozer with a touch of class that should be a bit of a secret to those in the know. It will have a gentle purr of contentment that goes with ale houses that need little advertisement, as they generate business by repeat trade. For me it is the place to start my town crawl if arriving via the Forster Square Station that is just around the corner.

BWV 1.3.06: Samuel Smith *OBB*

Bradford

Being Bradford based there is a danger this guide may be biased, but we will fight against getting angrier than usual. Bradford is big and was once rich, and had one of the worst bribe-fuelled concrete city centres in the country. Most of the worst buildings have been knocked down and for a brief time we can see the hills that made and surround the city. On a clear day there are stunning views down from the hills and up from the valley. What the view will be when the new buildings are up, we know not yet. The fact that our council has managed to turn Bradford Central Library from one of the finest in England to not even the best in Bradford, does not make us hopeful of quality or innovation.

Bradford does have three of the country's finest museums. The National Museum of Film, Photography and Television is rightly famous: The Colour Museum belongs to the Society of Dyers and Colourists and is a hidden gem near the Castle Hotel. Bradford City's own museum, in the back of the club's shop, is the best of its kind, and shows what a few enthusiastic fans can achieve in the face of club and council indifference.

Curries

Asians were working in Bradford's mills soon after WWII and opened curry houses to feed themselves. The natives took to them as well and many older Bradfordians, of whatever origin, eat their curries with a chapatti. Forks are for foreigners.

Brentford

Griffin Park is a homely ground in the middle of a large block of homely Edwardian housing, with the M4 to the north and the Thames to the south. We like it for that, but public transport links are as straightforward as complaining to a foreign call centre and driving a car here is probably harder than driving it to the top of Snowdon. If you have time there is much to see reasonably close to Griffin Park, but take a map, or plan your route beforehand.

Kew Gardens

The view depends on the season, but the Palm House, the Temperate House (biggest fancy greenhouse in the world), the People and Plants exhibition and The Marianne North Gallery, (one of the western worlds finest plant painters) are all out of the weather.

Kew Bridge Steam Museum

Opposite the Gardens and a mile east of Griffin Park, it has, possibly, the biggest steam pumping engine in the world, and a 'walk through sewer experience.' There is an entrance fee for this and the Gardens. *www.kbsm.org*

Hogarth's House

He was a great artist, a savage satirist and had an unmatched eye for the details of the human condition. His house has copies of many of his picture sets, including the Rake's Progress. This starts with the Rake getting his hands on his the family fortune, spending it foolishly, being made bankrupt, and finishing up as a madman in Bedlam; a story that is not based on modern football. The house is by *Chiswick Park.*

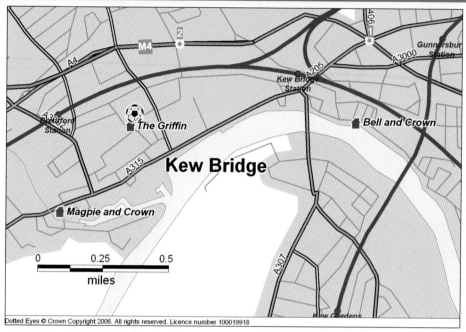

Kew Bridge

Bell and Crown

11-13 Thames Rd TW4 3PL. Telephone 02085 944164
Gaffers: Frank and Geraldine McBrearty
Food: High Quality menu, all freshly prepared to restaurant standard.
12 to 3, 6 to 9.30 in Winter, 12 to 9.30 Sun 12 to 8 in Summer
Separate smoking areas
Open: 11 to 11, 12 to 10.30 Sun

The Bell and Crown has one of the best riverside locations in London. From Kew Bridge you can see the pub and, no doubt, the crowds enjoying the walk to it when the sun shines. Geraldine and Frank run a top quality pub that has just been refurbished in the classic Fuller's style. The changes are very subtle and enhance the character of what is both a prime tourist location and a great local's food and ale house.

The best seats are in the conservatory where the full view of the river is found. The pub is, however, much more than just a show pub. It has several big areas around a central bar and the locals tend to use the front of the pub as the community meeting place. There are real fires to toast the chilled hands after a walk, and the welcome of the hosts is of the gentle warming Irish variety. The pub will be heaving on Twickenham related matchdays as it is also when the themed events are in full flow. Such was the case on my visit after the St Patrick's and Triple Crown days when the beer ran dry. The pub was sparkling; the river views fantastic and, as usual, a pint of ESB gave me the glad to be in London feeling. The eights toiled away in front of barking cyclists and pram - pushing parents, as I sat in the conservatory listening to London conversations. This is definitely the place for the family meal before a walk along the Thameside footpath to the ground.

BWV 22.3.06: Fuller's *Chiswick, ESB, London Pride*

The Griffin

Brook Road South TW8 0NP. Telephone 02085 608555 **New**

Gaffer: Ralph Clifton

Food: Good value, traditional pub food. BBQ in garden on match days 12 to 2

Smoking Throughout

Open: 11 to 12, 12 to 10.30 Sun

Doubtless many readers will know of, and will have visited, the Griffin before a game. It is the classic example of how Football and Real Ale works so well, sometimes without trying. This is because Ralph runs a pub that is geared up to the very best of stranger friendliness. It positively welcomes you to be part of the pub and the local Bees are the very best of friendly rivals. What will stand out on matchdays is the great friendly staff who know exactly how to get you a beer quickly and with a great smile.

| SP | SKY | JB | PG | D |

The pub is less than 50 metres from the away end and will be very busy. The garden plays a key function on matchdays by offering both an overflow area and barbeque food to fill the post-travel void. It is a classic community boozer, a sometime film set and a home to many groups of locals seeking a regular meeting place. On matchdays the pub becomes a base for all sorts of groups, from fanzine distributors to bucket collectors. The films include some classic big screen production, TV series and more recently adverts featuring Phil Taylor. The reason it is chosen is the classic London pub design. On my lunchtime visit the sun was streaming through the Fuller's etched windows into a room that is full of pub memorabilia. The pub itself is worth a visit, just to see why great community pubs such as this need some protection from redevelopment.

BWV 22.3 06: Fuller's *Discovery, London Pride*

Magpie and Crown

128 High Street, Brentford, TW8 8EW 02085 605658

Gaffer: Stephen Bolton

Food: Good quality, good value Thai food with comprehensive evening alternatives and set lunches 12 to 2.30 Mon, 12 to 2.30, 6 to 10 Tue to Sat, 12.30 to 6 Sun

Smoking Throughout

Open: 11 to 11 Mon to Wed, 11 to 12 Thu to Sat, 12 to 11 Sun

| SP | BM | PG |

The Magpie and Crown is a pub with a high regard for community activities, i.e. angling, beer, talking about London life, more beer, chat about the Broncos and the Bees, yet more beer. With an ever-changing list of rare ales to choose from (the board records 1420 in the landlord's time) the pub makes a refreshing change to the London scene so dominated by big pub tenancies. Add in foreign ales at relatively low prices, bottled ales and three real ciders, the choice for the true devotee is superb. This is the thinking man's pub even down to the Monday night board games.

UPDATE: Thai food is now available along with draft continental ales. The beer record now stands at 1590. Stephen has celebrated 10 years at this great institution and the themed beer selections continue to add some real interest for the regular ale-head. Note the cider choice in midwinter is increased as the season's demand and availability increases.

BWV 17.5.05: Welton's *Horsham Ruby Mild*, York *Mount Hood, Cascade, Guzzler*, Newton's *Discovery Cider*, Cirrus Minor *Cider*, Heart of Hampshire *Cider*

BWV 22.3.06: Crouch Vale *Brewers Gold*, Spinning Dog *Organic Bitter, Mutley's Revenge, Top Dog*, Gwatkins *Perry*

Plans are in place for you to be involved in writing for the Guides.
We already have a team of football fans who would like to share their experiences of drinking real ale when following their team.
I am offering a small payment to cover the cost of beer and transport when you research the pubs
You will not get rich doing this, neither will I
We would like you to join the team
It could be that you compile the entries for your own town
Maybe you might write about your favourites
You may even wish to rewrite my entries as they should be written
You can write as many or as little as we agree.

GO ON
JOIN THE TEAM

WRITE THE ALL NEW FOOTBALL AND REAL ALE GUIDES

JUST CONTACT ME
via email at r.stedman1@btinternet.com
OR by telephone at 01844 343931

THERE WILL NOT BE ANOTHER GUIDE UNLESS YOU HELP TO WRITE IT
THE 2007-08 GUIDES WILL BE EVEN BETTER FOR IT

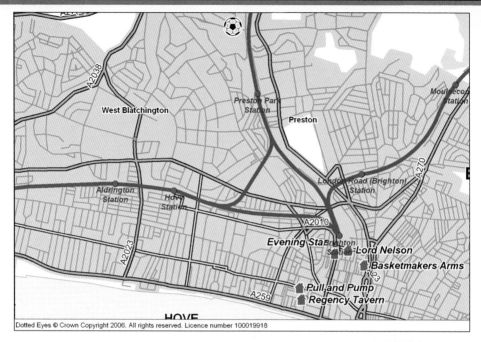

Basketmakers Arms

12 Gloucester Road, BN1 4AD. Telephone 01273 689006 **New**

Gaffer: Abi Mower

Food: Good wholesome homemade and local menu, often organic with daily specials 12 to 3, 5.30 to 8.30 Mon to Fri, 12 to 7 Sat, 12 to 5 Sun

Smoking Throughout

Open: 11 to 11, Mon to Wed, 11 to 12 Thu to Sat, 12 to 11 Sun

The Basketmakers has been highly recommended by first time readers of the guide who were amazed it wasn't in last year. I revisited and fell in love with it very quickly. This street corner pub is just perfect as the Brighton town local. It is full of quality features, most importantly being the ale selection and customer care.

MP – BM

I have to mention the décor. It is picture and postcard, antique and tobacco shop, waiting and living room all combined into a classic warm and friendly boozer. Then the food is both good quality and a good variation on the typical town pub fayre. There are some very special twists. Attached to the walls are hundreds of tobacco tins. Open them and you will find prophetic messages, often of the wise, or not so wise, to be read and or left. Don't be shy, the locals love seeing your reaction as you read them. Those locals are very much in the ready-rub and pipe smoking variety. The place was busy mid-afternoon with small groups of friends, mixed in sex and to a man, and woman, drinking pints. Perhaps that is why I was so smitten. If I lived here this would be my local. If a Brighton fan, then this is the definite starting point for the station based crawl. It will be busy on matchdays with people like you and me, standing room only maybe so get there early.

BWV 8.3.06: Fuller's *London Pride*, Gale's *Best, Butser, Festival Mild, HSB, Winter Brew*

Evening Star

55-56 Surrey Street, BN1 3PB. Telephone 01273 328931
www.theeveningstarbrighton.co.uk
Gaffers: Matt and Karen Wickham
Food: Rolls,12 to 3
Smoking Throughout
Open: 12 to 11 Sun to Thu, 12 to 12 Fri, 11.30 to 2 Sat and Sun

The Evening Star not only acts as the Dark Star Brewery tap but also champions local micro-brews This brick and wood-panelled bar very soon fills up with locals and regulars who wander from the offices and station to sample the variety that makes this place renowned. On matchdays expect a difficult search for a seat as it is the first or last port of call for the discerning real ale head. Add in a large list of European ales, no music or TV and you get a perfect real ale retreat for those who love quality as well as variety. Somehow live music also squeezes in on a Sunday evening. I sat near the window gazing at the street life outside and ear-wigging on Brighton conversation that drifted around the room. This is a top notch relaxing town boozer if ever there was one, a village local in the heart of the new city.

UPDATE: The pub has a sister in Shoreham, The Duke of Wellington is five mins from the station.

BWV 5.4.05: Dark Star *Hophead, Porter, APA (American Pale Ale)* Rother Valley *Hopper Ale, Special Edition,* Ryeburn *Luddite,* White *1066 Country Bitter,* Thatcher's *Black Rat Cider,* Weston's *Traditional Somerset Cider*
BWV 8.3.06: Archers *Fives and Threes,* Dark Star *American Pale Ale, Cathedral Stout, Hophead, Oatmeal Stout,* Everards *All Black,* Milestone *Hoptimism,* Thatcher's *Traditional, Cider,* Weston's *Traditional Scrumpy*

Lord Nelson

36 Trafalgar Street, BN1 4ED. Telephone 01273 695872
www.thelordnelsoninn.co.uk
Gaffer: Graham Boyd
Food: Special board and snack menu, all home cooked and locally sourced
12 to 2.30 Mon to Sat
Smoking Throughout
Open: 11 to 11, 11 to 10.30 Sun

This was a first for me, a pub which served the full range of Harveys ales in a pub that has bags of interest beyond the beer. The cellar awards proclaim the quality of the ales as do the recommendations of beer drinkers beyond Brighton. The pub has been creatively extended to include a gallery that hosts bi-monthly art exhibitions of local artists' work. The rest of the pub consists of three separate drinking areas one dominated by theatre and music posters, the front bar by memory-jerking photos related to the Albion. The best nook is the haunt of Seagulls echoing to the Goodbye Goldstone sentiment. This is a really friendly pub, instantly welcoming as you arrive and typically cosmopolitan in its outlook and clientele. As part of the Arts heritage trail and with fervent local CAMRA support, the Nelson holds a key place in the hearts of locals and visitors alike. This pub will get very busy on matchdays.

UPDATE: Sky TV is now a big screen in the bar that has had the carpets removed as part of an ongoing redecoration. Charity events and a Tuesday pub quiz now feature. The pub is still very good and still very busy.

BWV 5.4.05: Harveys *Armada, Best, IPA, Porter, Sussex Mild,* Addlestone's *Cider*
BWV 8.3.06: Harveys *Armada, Best, IPA, Old Ale, Porter, Sussex Mild,* Addlestone's *Cider*

Pull and Pump

1 Clarence Gardens, BN1 2EG Telephone 01273 328263. www.pleisure.com
Gaffer: Helen Rudd
Food: Traditional home-cooked menu to suit all tastes 12 to 3, Mon to Sun
Smoking Throughout
Open: 12 to 11 Sun to Thu, 12 to 12 Fri and Sat

The Pleisure group is an interesting additional to the pub groups of the South East, and a cursory glance at their website gives clues as to the atmosphere you would expect to find in their pubs. The emphasis is on good fun in proper pubs and the Pull and Pump is a great example of this. It also has a good choice of ales, in a location that is great, and being near the Regency makes it my choice for those who venture well away from the station. The fun is evident in the curious choice of special evenings. Geared up for the more youthful is the "Spelling Bee" held monthly. The alcohol offers are of the spiritual variety. You will now be imagining the worst of a fun pub. Would I do that to you? The pub is a proper pub with a relaxed and welcoming atmosphere. Helen has built up a great reputation with ale drinkers and encourages gentle humour and quiet conversation.

The pub is a single-roomed, timber-floored tavern, with the large windows I always imagined would be common-place in Brighton pubs. The view from the window is of a Regency street scene and, for wicked amusement, traffic wardens cruising for easy pickings. My afternoon visit found many younger couples enjoying a late lunch. The local characters were starting to arrive and start up bar-fly style chat. It was all very safe and cheerful, and what's more there was HSB as guest ale.

BWV 8.3.06: Gale's *HSB*, Harveys *Best*, Shepherd Neame *Spitfire*, Young's *Special*

Regency Tavern

32-34 Russell Square, BN1 2EF. Telephone 01273 325652
www.shepherdneame.co.uk
Gaffer: James Brett
Food: All home-made menu with ever-changing specials
12 to 2.30 Mon to Sat, 12 to 3 Sun
Smoking Throughout
Open: 11 to 11 Sun to Thu, 11 to 12 Fri and Sat

A trip to Brighton should include a walk on the seafront and a pint to follow. One should also admire the Regency architecture and then taste local ales. Therefore the Regency gets my vote as the perfect pub of this type. The Regency is the definition of anachronistic. Its fame among locals comes from the interior décor, all silhouettes, busts and swirling drapes. Then the pub has a disco theme to suggest a lively history and future. The pub is very comfortable, relaxing and a true treasure that the recent change of ownership will apparently cherish. This is a destination pub at weekends; people find it hard to leave once inside. The local urban architecture gives clues to its regulars, sixties apartments mix with the affluent regency mansions. Between town and the sea the best time to visit is the hot summer day or early evening when the calm of the shade it provides and the quality of the ale would make for heavenly refreshment.
UPDATE: The repainting of the exterior is complete and the plan is to redecorate inside are still plans. The meals are likely to change to include two course specials and home made desserts. The pub is essentially as it was last year.

BWV 5.4.05: Shepherd Neame *Best, Bishops Finger, Early Bird, Spitfire*.
BWV 8.3.06: Shepherd Neame *Bishop's Finger, Early Bird, Kents Best, Spitfire*

Brighton

Brighthelmston was a fishing village that once drove the press gang away using the head breaking, feet crippling rocks from the 'beach'. Some can walk barefoot on hot coals and some can walk barefoot on Brighton beach. Visitors first came here to drink spring water in Hove. When bathing in, and drinking the sea became fashionable, the village became Brighton and boomed.

The Royal Pavilion

Finished in 1821 for the Prince Regent/George IV, the great Sydney Smith said of it; 'Brighton Pavilion looks as if St. Paul's had come down and littered.' William Cobbett described it as a; 'square box, a large Norfolk turnip and four onions.'

brighton-hove.gov.uk/bhc/pavilion

Brighton Museum and Art Gallery

This quirky and old fashioned museum used to be one of the best in Britain. It has now suffered a £10 million make-over. The Evening Argus site said it is; 'Dynamic and innovative... utilising the latest interactive technology.' So it will be full of things that break down, which tax eating bureaucrats can show off to other empire builders who shamelessly use words like 'interactive.'

Sea Life Centre

We like Sea Life Centres. The best things are the skates and rays. They normally stay flat on the sea bottom, but in captivity act like puppies: sticking their front ends out of the water and flapping their wings until someone tickles them. Visitors were warned not to touch them, but the fish obviously enjoy it: why is a deeper question!

Bristol City

The phrases West Country and big city have probably not run together in many people's minds; but for a long time Bristol was Britain's second city. By one measure it was still England's sixth largest in 2001.

Bristol grew rich from trade, and later also from industry. Wealth came from wool, slaving, and then fag making. Bristol was rich when people spent their money where they made it. Bristol has the marvellous Cathedral and wonderful church of St. Mary Redcliffe: as well as later Georgian developments: but Bristol also has grim areas, even in the centre. Temple Meads Station's surroundings were amongst the shabbiest in England, but we guess it has been gentrified.

Clifton Suspension Bridge and the SS Great Britain

Built by Brunel it looks grand, attracts tourists: but was immense trouble to make, never made money and caused bankruptcies; catastrophic failures by any sane measure. The bridge took 28 years to build and was completed using second hand chains. The ship was built as an Atlantic liner, failed and did increasingly lowly jobs before being abandoned in the Falklands like a burnt-out 'twocked' car behind a council estate.

Bristol Zoo

A varied but not over big zoo, we mention it especially to call for a Johnny Morris revival. He filmed Animal Magic here, and it was magic: but his best work was on radio. We were told that he always went into the studio with a briefcase, which turned out to be full of beer rather than scripts. What a star!

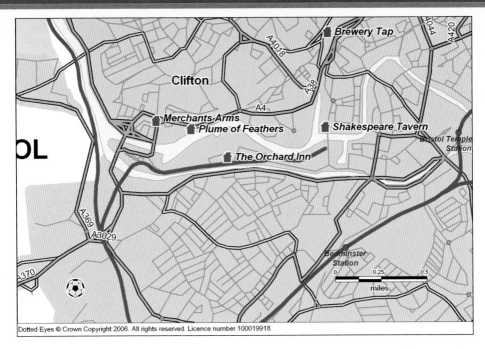

Brewery Tap

Upper Maudlin Street, BS1 5BD. Telephone 0117 9213668
Gaffer: Emma Marlton
**Food: Good quality traditional pub menu 12 to 2.30, 6 to 9 Mon to Fri,
12 to 2.30 Sat, No food Sun**
Separate smoking areas
Open: 12 to 11.30

Smiles brewing may have joined Courage as being lost to Bristol but the Smiles
Company Brewery Tap continues the traditions of this innovative and much-loved
Bristol beer trend setter. Other local ales will undoubtedly come to take
prominence over the months but the comfort and originality of this pub continues to be popular with people of all
ages and outlooks. My lunchtime visit found mostly women in the bar; nurses, office meetings, groups of people taking
a drink between the town and tourist business. The layout means that you can usually find solitude in one of the back
wooden-walled rooms or join in more pubby chat at the bar at the front. I like the use of hop sacks on the wall and
the general feeling of well planned disorganisation within the rustic furniture. This is a gentle lunchtime pub that gives
way to young and old planning nights out in town in the evening. It is a great pub in a good location and with, one
hopes, a bright, if now less Smiles dependent, future.
UPDATE: Emma has taken charge at the pub and brings a wide knowledge of Bristol pub life.

BWV 12.4.05 Smiles *Heritage, Best, Bristol IPA,* Wickwar *Cotswold Way*
BWV 1.6.06: Ramsbury *Spring Barley,* Smiles *Best, Heritage, Jarrow Irish Stout,* Moles *Black Rat Cider,*
Thatcher's *Dry Cider*

Merchants Arms

Merchants Road, Hotwells, BS8 9PZ. Telephone 0117 9040037 **New**

Gaffer: John Lansdall

Food: Specialist pies and pasties when open

Smoking Throughout

Open: 12 to 2.30, 5 to 11 Mon to Sat, 12 to 10.30 Sun

The Merchants is probably the smallest of the Bristol Bath Ales pubs and has a place in the pub landscape for its location and great design. It was converted into the present shape just six years ago but it is so considerately done that one would never know that the pub isn't in the same state as when the local dock workers would have frequented it in Bristol's' maritime heyday.

The pub is really one small bar separated into two sections, the rear being a snug, the front a slightly larger bar. It is wood-panelled, and floored, with large picture windows through which one can watch the commuters crawling towards the nearby Cumberland Basin intersection. The locals are as legendary as the Split Tin pies and pasties. While the locals return, apparently the food often runs out by the weekend. Take care however, because this information was supplied by a local who only wanted to be known by his membership of the British Interplanetary Society. John's pub is just a ten minute walk from Ashton Gate but is in a totally different world from that found south of the river. The sun certainly shines on the Hotwells area if you want a large choice of ale houses. The Merchants represents the best of a very good bunch. The Notts County fans who recommended the pub were correct in picking it as a place that will get full very quickly but is somewhere that makes the visit to Bristol somewhat different. The wheelbarrow was apparently full of ale and pasties on that day.

BWV 26.11.05: Bath Ales *Barnstormer, Festivity, Gem, Spa*

Plume of Feathers

135 Hotwell Road, Hotwells BS8 4RU. Telephone 0117 929866 **New**

www.plumeoffeathers.com

Gaffer: Mark Farrell

Food: Wonderful café style food including specials and salads.

9 to 2 Mon to Fri, 9.30 to 2 Sat, 9.30 to Midday Sunday lunches 12 to 4

Separate smoking areas

Open: 11 to 11 (café open at 9)

The Hotwells triangle is the ultimate destination for those seeking ale in Bristol yet wanting to avoid the typical city-centre evening experience. The Feathers is well-established, well known by both tourists and Bristolian alike. I arrived early to find a steady stream of locals arriving for '*a full English*' before opening, Anne has a good café going on here that attracts the office crowd and also acts as a stop-off point for those who use the water taxi to come and go to the city centre. Add in a upstairs function room with views across the harbour to the SS Great Britain and you know that the pub will make a good impression. It is a simple one-room bar with a cracking atmosphere favoured by Swifty, my press friend, and is noted for the friendliness of the locals. On matchdays the pub will not be full of City fans but those who do drink here are will be real-ale-heads enjoying the selection and regular cider that supplements the choice. In the summer it is the base for the Black Sheep rowing team taking part in the Avon Rowing Regatta. It also plans to hold a real ale festival in February 2006. This is a great town boozer. Mark knows what his locals need, i.e. students with little money are as valued as the young professionals hiking up and down the hill from Clifton.

BWV 26.11.05: Adnams *Broadside*, Bass *Draught*, Black Sheep *Bitter*, Butcombe *Bitter*, Highgate *Dark Mild*, Timothy Taylor *Landlord*, Weston's *Organic Cider*

The Orchard Inn

Hanover Place, BS1 6XT Telephone 0117 9262678 **New**

Gaffer: Rob Merchant

Food: Good value traditional pub food 12 to 2 Mon to Fri

Smoking Throughout

Open: 12 to 3, 5 to 11 Mon to Sat, 12 to 3, 7 to 10.30 Sun

The Orchard Inn represents all that is really good in a typical Bristol town boozer. It is small, instantly welcoming and has managed to adapt as all around it has changed in the last twenty years. This is due in part to the landlord having a history of not only being here for seventeen years but also his father being the boss before him.

SP | BM | D

Spike Island, the area between the river and Feeder canal has been transformed from the heart of the Bristol docklands to a rather trendy and certainly gentrified enclave that has a great mix of long-established locals and youngish professionals living the planners' dream. The pub is small, having a street corner location that allows light to enter on both sides. It has an outside drinking space which was very popular on my brief summer afternoon visit. The interior is very much in the living room style. It is subdivided by a clever, raised and railed off, area but essentially it is small enough for conversation to be pub-wide. Do not expect to find hoards of football fans, it is too remote and off the obvious routes to the ground. Do expect to come across regulars, both City and Rovers supporters, who mix happily, enjoying a healthy rivalry not always found city-wide. The Orchard is one of the few remaining freehouses in the city and long may it stay exactly as it is, a proper pub that is the centre of a city-wide real ale drinking community.

BWV 1.6.06: Bath Ales *Gem*, Butcombe *Bitter*, Sharp's *Doom Bar*, Moles *Black Rat Cider*, Thatcher's *Cheddar Valley, Traditional Somerset Cider*

Shakespeare Tavern

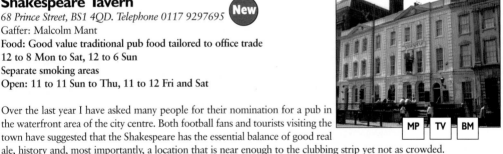

68 Prince Street, BS1 4QD. Telephone 0117 9297695 **New**

Gaffer: Malcolm Mant

Food: Good value traditional pub food tailored to office trade

12 to 8 Mon to Sat, 12 to 6 Sun

Separate smoking areas

Open: 11 to 11 Sun to Thu, 11 to 12 Fri and Sat

Over the last year I have asked many people for their nomination for a pub in the waterfront area of the city centre. Both football fans and tourists visiting the town have suggested that the Shakespeare has the essential balance of good real

MP | TV | BM

ale, history and, most importantly, a location that is near enough to the clubbing strip yet not as crowded.

Malcolm has only been here a few months and he has already re-established the traditions of creating a proper ale house in this impressive 18th century building. The interior has all the elements of a nautically designed hostelry. The two rooms are timber panelled and have masses of references to Bristol long gone. The regulars are an interesting mix of local office workers and, almost unique to Bristol, people who live on the water. This is quite a trendy thing to do in this city. The evening also has its fair smattering of arty folk heading for the Arnolfini nearby or sampling an ale before venturing across the footbridge to events in the new '*Cultural Zone*.' Malcolm is also a football fan of the truly mixed up variety that goes with being a pub landlord. He has allegiances to Devon football and Arsenal, how sad is that! On my lunchtime visit I got the distinct impression that banter is free- flowing. The outside terrace was very popular with lunchtime drinkers, doubtless this is also true late into the night. With good hotels nearby no wonder it is popular with my visiting friends.

BWV 1.6.06: Greene King *Abbot, IPA, Old Speckled Hen, Ruddles County*

Need print?
We tackle everything

Expertise in Print & Design
☎ 01454 319555

TL Visuals Limited

TL Visuals Ltd, Armstrong Way, Yate, Bristol, BS37 5NG
Tel. 01454 319555

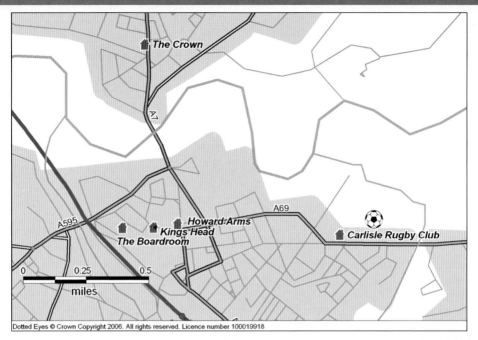

Dotted Eyes © Crown Copyright 2006. All rights reserved. Licence number 100019918

The Boardroom

Paternoster Row, CA3 8TT. Telephone 01228 527695 **New**

Gaffer: David Scott

Food: Simple pub food from sandwiches to steaks 12 to 2, not Sun

Separate smoking areas

Open: 11 to 12, 12 to 2, 7 to 10.30 Sun

The Boardroom is the recommendation of my companion for the North East trip. Ray was bowled over by the location, the history and the overall enthusiasm of David, the landlord of 17 years. I had to agree the Boardroom offers something more than that found in other town-centre pubs.

The location is truly impressive; the picture window in which we sat had picturesque early spring views of the cathedral across the road, the connections apparently being via underground tunnels as well as the more mundane pelican. This historical element extends to a resident ghost? Dave is keen to let you know about this and also the story of Doris and the ale that is also resident on the beer list. The pub is a largish extended one-room bar, as impressive as the listed façade that is prominent as tourists walk between town station, cathedral and church. Those tourists will be very evident is summer. On our winter visit the locals held the prime locations, i.e. the seats made of church pew ends complete with umbrella stand ends. The typical clientele is a mix of office workers and students, shoppers and Scots escaping to the nearest English town. The pub offers no music, TV or loud lads' conversation. It is very much the place for that quiet pub lunch and relief from the crowds milling along the Warwick Road before a game.

BWV 8.2.06: Hesket Newmarket *Doris' 90th Birthday Ale*, Theakston's *Best*

Carlisle Rugby Club

Warwick Road, CA1 1CW. Telephone: 01228 521300 **New**
Gaffer: Bill Swarbrick
Food: Rolls and sandwiches by arrangement, to groups who phone ahead
Separate smoking areas
Open: 7 to 11, 12 to 11 Sat, 12 to 3, 7 to 11 Sun

| CP | SKY | D |

To understand the full effects of the floods one needs only to spend an hour chatting to the locals of Warwick Road who also use the local rugby Club. The water rose to the height of the cross bar, i.e. near to the ceiling of the room as marked behind the bar. Some will talk of good fortune; this has provided an opportunity to rebuild and in parts to redesign the bar which now has a modern clubhouse feeling and extended bar space.

The Carlisle Rugby Club has long been a favourite of mine because it has always offered the best alternative beers in the town. The friendliness is infectious, i.e. those who use it are very loyal to the place and rarely venture in to town either before or after. There are two rooms, one is non-smoking. New plasma screens should be noted, especially as the international rugby games will take priority, and rightly so. The pub is closed during weekdays and I was indeed very fortunate to meet up with Dave in the Howard Arms. Typical of those who run the club, he was more than helpful in pointing out some of the vagaries of the rugby scene. The place hosts a squash club, as well as having very close ties with United. The team is presently at the top of their league and would love some more locals to support the club. When football is in town there is an unwritten law, however, that the rugby game starts just as away fans head across the park to the game.

BWV 8.2.06: Goose Eye *No Eye Deer*, Theakston's *Best*, Yates' *Bitter*

The Crown

23 Scotland Road, Stanwix CA3 9HS. Telephone 01228 512789
Gaffer: Paul White
Food: Good value meals and sandwiches including steaks from £3.95,
12 to 7.30
Separate smoking areas and not at the bar
Open: 11.30 to 11

| SP | SKY | JB | PG | D |

The Crown is a large street-corner pub on the way north out of the town. It is a good local that supports a pub team. Not loads of real ale, but enough to subtly point them away from the smooth stuff. Paul is a Carlisle season ticket holder and appreciates that the locals like their sport. The TV screen was tuned to afternoon racing, I left as the pub favourite missed out on a punters' reward. It is 75% non smoking, yet large enough for those who wished to play pool, drink ale and do normal pubby activities. Designed in the wood panelled library style it suits the younger as well as more mature, drinker; so too those seeking food. Apparently the local CAMRA crew have been sighted and one would think it would make a good addition to their guide. A taxi or 15 minute walk from the ground and town, the Crown offers an alternative to suit both ale heads and your mate who hasn't yet seen the light.
UPDATE: The pub has changed ownership in the Punch/Spirit dealing. Otherwise all is the same. The best place to park is across the road, and then walk along the river.

BWV 18.5 05: Theakston's *Best*, Wadworth *Summersault*
BWV 8.2.06: Holt *Bitter*, Theakston's *Best*

Howard Arms

107 Lowther Street, CA3 8ED. Telephone 01228 532926
Gaffer: Harry Ross
Food: Traditional pub food and bar lunches 12 to 2, not Sun
No smoking at the bar
Open: 11 to 11, 11 to 10.30 Sun

MP | SKY | JB | D

Graham, Lawrence and Ian, doing the whistle stop tour from Newcastle, pointed me in the direction of this pub from the Cumberland Arms. It has connections with the long-gone theatre opposite and, by a quirk of fate, the unearthed ornate tiled frontage now helps to guarantee its historical importance.
As a real ale pub, Harry runs a rarity, a great town centre pub with character, and a locals' boozer The pub started with and keeps its original cosiness, the extensions to the rear have only created more small rooms and an outside patio equally compact in size. The locals were fantastic, old boys talking of the season to come, walkers staggering in off the Hadrian's walk to sup thirst-quenching ale, even a ladies circle could be heard discussing which pub to meet in next week. It was busy on my lunchtime visit and very friendly. It is Harry's 21st birthday as landlord here and the pub is obviously well loved. It appeared to be very much a gentlepersons' club, refined yet a place to enjoy.
UPDATE: The guest ale is always changing. It was great to meet with Dave Burnett of Carlisle Rugby Club here this year.

BWV 18.5 05: Theakston's *Best*, *XB*
BWV 8.2.06: Theakston's *Best*, Wells *Bombardier*

Kings Head

Fisher Street, CA3 8RF. Telephone: 01228 533797
Gaffer: Mike Vose
Food: Traditional pub food 10 to 3, 11 to 3 Sat, No food Sun
Separate smoking areas
Open: 10 to 11, 11 to 11 Sat, 12 to 10.30 Sun

MP | TV | BM | PG | D

Mike is a Cumbrian Gooner who has a passion for liberating the locals from smooth land to real ale. As such the Kings Head is the only pub in the town centre to offer genuine local ales, i.e. Yates', and a guest that is ever-changing. The Kings Head is smack bang in tourist and shopper land, yet has a real locals following. The regulars were gathered around the bar talking of last weekend's triumphs in Stoke, often bemoaning the lack of quality real ale there. The pub is a carpeted, timber-roofed tavern that extends deep to the rear where the best sitting and chatting space is found. And so it was that I found my final new pub of the year, several weeks later than planned. Matt and the locals were great company, as is the case whenever you come into this pub. They shared tales of away fans and pubs in the Conference and dreams of beer hunting this season, good times! The renaissance of Carlisle town centre real ale, I predict, will start here. As it grows give Mike your support, you know it makes sense.
UPDATE: A heated outside garden may be in place sometime next year.

BWV 8.2.06: Fuller's *London Pride*, Yates' *Bitter*
BWV 18.5.05: The Old Mill *Bullion*, Yates' *Bitter*

CULTURAL GUIDES

Carlisle

Long before England and Scotland existed, groups of blokes were carrying war and raping to, or from, the North. Carlisle blocked the easier, West Coast route. The Roman fort, and later castle were built on a hill for protection and a view: but it could be supplied by the sea while the Solway Firth remained navigable. Carlisle Castle remained in garrison use well after the physical wars between Scotland and England had ended, but now seems to be just for tourists. The sea has long abandoned the town as well, even though rain and tides have occasionally returned with a vengeance.

Carlisle tried to retain sea access in the early 19th Century by building Port Carlisle 15 miles down the Firth. It had a canal; then a railway which, for most of its life, had one passenger carriage, pulled by one horse. So obviously it was not a thriving port. It is now a hamlet near Bowness-on-Solway, the site of western end of Hadrian's Wall: and also the virtually forgotten Solway Viaduct. This was over a mile long, linked the two countries, and was demolished in 1934.

Carlisle still has a sense of grandeur and drama, best appreciated if you arrive by train. The station is vast and is on English Street. It is faced by the Citadel, built in Henry VIII time, and behind that the street runs to the Old Town Hall, now a tourist office, and becomes Scotch Street. All the historic buildings are close by.

Cheltenham

This Georgian town grew on the combined obsessions with class, status and health that make England such a friendly and relaxed country.

The idea that water that springs from the ground is special when compared to 'ordinary' water, has deep roots. People have long visited springs to be 'cured'. The original excuse was because they were holy: but with the early stumbling growth of chemistry and medicine came the replacement excuse that certain, generally vile tasting, spring waters might contain health giving chemicals. Thus the Belgium town of Spa has flourished for over 500 years; and Cheltenham is one of England's more successful copies.

Cheltenham's official tourist myth is that the original spring was discovered because of pigeons gathering for a salt lick. *The Spa* was developed from 1738 by one Henry Skillicone, who gained the land by marriage and made his fortune as a sea captain, a trade as full of honest men then as football club ownership is now. He certainly made Cheltenham into a profitable place, with the usually mercenary expert writing a book about how the water would cure everything but the urge to spend money on chasing fashion. A visit by George III and some of the less frightful members of his family wetted the appetites of snobs. *Skillicone's gravestone*, inside Cheltenham's church, is as long as a first novel by a television personality, but better written. It stops short of claiming he invented the wheel and could fly, but only just.

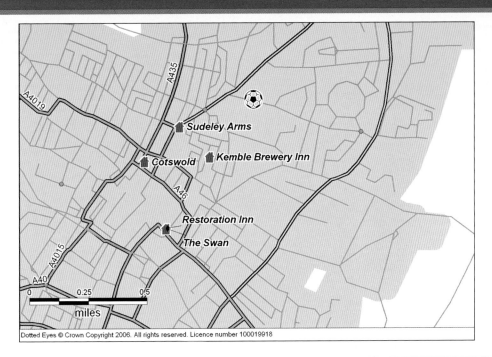

Dotted Eyes © Crown Copyright 2006. All rights reserved. Licence number 100019918

Cotswold

17 Portland Street, GL52 2NZ. Telephone 01242 525570
Gaffers: John and Clare Freeman
Food: Good pub grub with American style burger specialities
7 to 9 Mon to Thu, 12.30 to 2.30 Fri to Sun
Smoking Throughout
Open: 12 to 12

This pub is on the up. One for the younger ale drinker it offers something very different to the traditional real ale house. '*Good simple food in a grungy atmosphere, or quality music in the cellar bar, it is a refreshing change to the Cheltenham norm.*' My visit included a tour of the downstairs bar where it isn't difficult to imagine the attraction of this place to those who like their music loud, live and lively. I was also tempted by the apparently well priced and good quality pub grub. As A. Stinton of Cheltenham says '*It is a friendly, open pub where you can always find a good atmosphere. Compared to the majority of the pubs in the town it certainly shines out as the most relaxed and enjoyable.*' This was my experience as some pubs, that I will not name, not only declined to discuss the footie and real ale phenomena but were unusually arrogant in their opinion that they had no need to publicise their qualities. I will not then.

UPDATE: Live music is upstairs leaving the cellar to Heavy Metal fans. In the next year the aim is for the pub to become the Cheltenham Steak pub. The beer is still excellent, offering occasional guest ale. The CAMRA folk still meet here, those crazy quotas strike again.

BWV 29.12.04: Wadworth *6X, Henry's IPA, Old Timer*
BWV 13.1.06: Wadworth *6X, Henry's IPA, Old Timer*

Kemble Brewery Inn

27 Fairview Street GL52 2JF. Telephone 01242 243446
Gaffer: Eileen Melia
Food: Good pub grub specialising in chillies, curries and breakfast meals from 12 to 2
Smoking Throughout
Open: 12 to 2.30, 5.30 to 11.30

This pub is nowhere near Kemble, a Gloucestershire village more famous for plane spotting than the brewery that used to produce cider for the ex landlord of this pub. Very crowded on match days this is a traditional community pub that sets the standard for Cheltenham. Eileen, the landlady looks after regulars and new friends really well in a pub that is like your grannies front room with piano and TV to boot. The pub has a beer garden for summer games and always has two beers different to the high quality IPA and Timmy Taylor. *'This pub always wins awards for being simply the best.'* Every visit has found people newly discovering the Kemble and wondering why every back - street pub near a ground can't be as good as this. The food is simple pub grub, the atmosphere is positively bubbly, the chances of getting a seat minimal, unless you get there early. Never mind, stand by the piano and talk ale.
UPDATE A canopy over the beer garden will provide space should the smoking laws change. Resident parking is in place but it is still difficult to park.

BWV 29.12.04: Brakspear *O Be Joyful*, Greene King *IPA*, Smiles *Bristol IPA*, Timothy Taylor *Landlord*, Whittington's *Cat's Whiskers*, Wye Valley *Hereford Pale Ale*
BWV 13.1.06: Bath Ales *Spa*, Black Sheep *Special*, Fuller's *London Pride*, Timothy Taylor *Landlord*, Whittington *Cat's Whiskers*, Wye Valley *Hereford Pale Ale*

Restoration Inn

New

55-57 High Street, GL50 1DX. Telephone 01242 522792
Gaffers: Ian and Tracy Newbold
Food: Good value, varied menu in the traditional pub food style
Separate smoking areas
Open: 11 to 11, 12 to 11 Sun.

One aim of the widened scope of this years' guides was to get some more youthful High Street locations. This Barracuda pub offers such a location, great ale selections and a friendliness that encourages younger drinkers to sample real ale. As a C15th pub it claims to be the towns oldest but the interior is of the now classic, split-level, open-plan design. There will always be between two and six ales. The regulars sit at the bar while couples venture deep into the rear of this large pub. It is more likely that you will find local Rugby fans/players than football supporters. As the retiring postman said *'What I like is that Ian knows what I want to drink and is willing to get involved in bar-fly chat.'*

The food is in the *'platter'* style that attracts family eating on the cheap, the beer is of the independent style that attracts beer tickers like me. One observation is that for once I was the eldest at the bar, 80% of those locals wearing hats, curious! It is not a rowdy place nor will the chain pub youths like this place; but as a pub to take the girlfriend and enjoy predictable youthful chat then this is the pub to hang out during the evening. As a new entry to the local CAMRA guide, the Restoration is a good honest town-centre pub. I just wish all such redesigned pubs were like this.

BWV 13.1.06: St. Austell *Tinners*, *Tribute*, Wickwar *Cotswold Way*, Wychwood *Hobgoblin*, Wye Valley *Bitter*

Sudeley Arms

25 Prestbury Road, GL52 2PN. Telephone 01242 510687
Gaffer: Gary Hyett
Smoking Throughout
Open: 11 to 11.30, 12 to 10.30 Sun.

The Sudeley is the archetypal *'potential'* pub; the three rooms are off a central bar. Gary caters for a wide range of locals, workers and event visitors. He has created a sporting bias with local teams, pub games and a generally welcoming feel. *'Look out for cider from the bin and the pub dog.'* It deserves your custom because *'it is rare in Cheltenham to find a real pub with real values of good service'* to the regulars and visitors alike. I really enjoyed the public bar, of traditional design and atmosphere. The locals chat is often related to horse racing rather than the Robins; well their league status is somewhat shorter than the festival. I can imagine this pub being very popular during Cheltenham week so too when the pub gets its regulars into party mode. It is a short walk to the ground, so I would park up near the ground and walk back for a long leisurely pint, with food taken from nearby chippies or at the ground. The welcome is good, the company just fine. *UPDATE:* This is the same friendly local, well recommended by away fans because of its easy walk to the ground and as the last leg of the town to ground crawl.

BWV 29.12.04: Camerons **Castle Eden Ale**, Goff's **Jouster**, Timothy Taylor **Landlord**
BWV 13.1.06: Brains **SA**, Goff's **Jouster**, Timothy Taylor **Landlord**, Young's **Special**, Weston's **Old Rosie**

The Swan

37 High Street, GL50 1DX. Telephone 01242 584989 **New**
www.theswan-cheltenham.co.uk
Gaffers: Steven and Becky Hall
Food: Restaurant food, freshly prepared to order in traditional British pub style all day,12.30 to 4 weekends
Separate smoking areas
Open: 12 to 11 Mon to Thu, 12 to 12 Fri and Sat, 12 to 10.30 Sun

The Swan is the towns' CAMRA Pub of the Year and seeing the choice of ales that are ever-changing it is easy to understand that choice. Steven and Becky have created a touch of *'capital class'* in their short time at the pub. The team includes Rosie, Dan and Vanda who run a great pub with customer service to die for. For example, I was pleasantly surprised to be offered a choice of straight or jug. Groups of young women with young children were obviously welcome, there is plenty enough space for all as the pub extends deep to the rear off the High Street.

The atmosphere is perhaps best described as convivial. Fun also comes to mind as one notes that it hosts *'speed-dating, great live music and fab' real ales.'* Hopefully they don't run simultaneously! You should never rush ale of this quality. The pub will get comfortably busy on matchdays but you are more likely to find cricket and rugby fans. Those wanting big screen action will be in the Restoration along the road. The rear beer garden also looked tempting for those hot summer evenings. The pub oozes sophistication without losing those essentials of intimacy for the locals who like their regular corners. I am sure you can find whatever you want in one of the four distinct drinking areas. For me it would be the front bar, enjoying a view of the traffic jams outside.

BWV 13.1.06: Battledown **Saxon**, Hidden Brewery **Hidden Quest**, Sharp's **Cornish Coaster**

TAXIS

This page gives one taxi company in each town. There is no recommendation as to their reliability. They are taken from random internet searches for taxis in the town and then chosen by these criteria:

• I may have used them on my travels. I usually ask a landlord to recommend a cab company

• Based in the town centre or near the station

• Large enough to be able to afford advertising nationally

• The first I came across if the above are not immediately found

I know this is a bit subjective but I often suggest getting a taxi to the ground so it would be remiss of me not to offer some numbers.

	Taxi	Number	
BLACKPOOL	Gold line	01253	590500
BOURNEMOUTH	AAA	0800	654321
BRADFORD	Barkerend	01274	391676
BRENTFORD	Brentford and Ealing Radio	02088	406699
BRIGHTON	Streamline	01273	747474
BRISTOL C	Alpha	01179	211211
CARLISLE	Beeline	01228	534440
CHELTENHAM	Central	01242	228877
CHESTERFIELD	Central	01246	200500
CREWE	Premier	01270	582020
DONCASTER	Dial a cab	01302	323737
GILLINGHAM	Star	01634	575656
HUDDERSFIELD	ABC Taxis	01484	546333
LEYTON ORIENT	Midland	02085	390127
MILLWALL	Excel	02084	690104
NORTHAMPTON	A1	01604	627777
NOTTINGHAM F	Clifton	01159	143143
OLDHAM	Borough	01616	287777
PORT VALE	City cabs 2000	01782	844444
ROTHERHAM	Milennium	01709	382838
SCUNTHORPE	Alpha	01724	343434
SWANSEA	High Street	01792	477477
TRANMERE	Oz cabs	01516	661511
YEOVIL	ABC	01935	477770

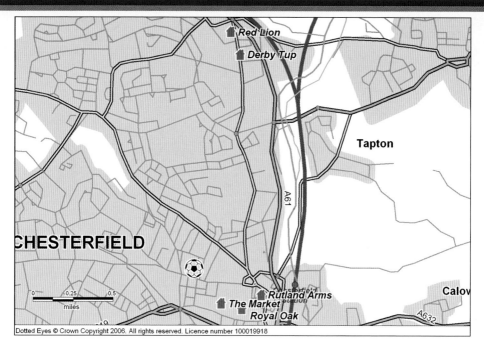

Dotted Eyes © Crown Copyright 2006. All rights reserved. Licence number 100019918

Derby Tup

387 Sheffield Road, S40 8LS Telephone 01246 454316
www.thederbytup@tiscali.com
Gaffer: Brendan McConville
Food: Hot baguettes and snack food 12 to 2
Separate smoking areas
Open:11.30 to 3, 5 to 11 Mon to Thu, 11.30 to 12 Fri and Sat,
12 to 11.30 Sun

The No. 25 bus took me to the famous Derby Tup and it is a must if you are to sample the best. I was not alone on my visit. There are three separate rooms, the smallest snug designated as non-smoking. I preferred the longer central bar where wooden tables and chairs arranged around the walls made for instant cross-group chat. The locals raved about the qualities of the Tup. No music, no juke box, no gimmicks; just quality ale and the essential ingredient, great regulars who have made the pub what it is. The conversation roams from ales onto politics and sport and then back to the ale. This is Chesterfields pub of the year, it would stand it's ground in any town in the country, I would love this to be my local. Go on, £1.80 return will be the best investment of the day.
UPDATE: Watch out for the Beer Festival at the end of September.

BWV 24.3.05: Burton Bridge *Porter*, Bateman *XXXB*, Everards *Perfick*, Newby Wyke *Bear Island*, Oakham *JHB*, Oldershaw *Isaacs Gold*, Timothy Taylor *Landlord*, Wards *Best*, Rudgate *Earls Ale*, Weston's *Old Rosie*, Biddenden *Dry*, *Medium Ciders*, Broadoak *Moonshine Cider*
BWV 11.5.06: Bateman *XXXB*, Burton Bridge *Porter*, Caledonian *Dr Bob's Mild*, Copper Dragon *Golden Pippin*, Scotts *1816*, Libra *On Balance*, Newby Wyke *New Wave*, Titanic *Iceberg*, Timothy Taylor *Landlord*

The Market

95 New Square S40 1AH. Telephone 01246 27364 **New**

Gaffer: Keith Toone

Food: All home made and home cooked food in the traditional English pub food style 11 to 2.30

Separate smoking areas

Open: 11 to 11 Mon to Sat, 7.30 to 10.30 Sun

The Market is a classic market-square pub of the very traditional style. I visited on a market day and saw it at its brilliant best, very busy, chatty and homely all at the same time.

The pub has everything, quite literally. Good beers and interesting guest ales are supped in either a timber floored bar, a flag stoned area or over a meal in the carpeted lounge. All have low ceilings and rely on natural light through the feature leaded windows to the front of the bar. I shared the pub session with some good old boys avoiding the market scrummage and generally older couples obviously having their weekly meal out in their favourite town location. The food is very important on these days. In the evenings the regulars are more likely to be the real ale fans, again of the more mature variety than is often found in a typical market town centre. On a match day there are unlikely to be many Chesterfield fans the football fans will be visiting real ale heads enjoying the friendliness of the pub. I retired to the small courtyard garden where the kitchen could be seen in full frenzy. The younger female luncheoners were here and to be honest I enjoyed eavesdropping on life in the '*Spire*' town. I really enjoyed this pub, the younger real ale heads will maybe find it a bit too traditional.

BWV 11.5.06: Greene King *Abbot*, Marston's *Pedigree*, Robinson's *Unicorn*, Spire *Encore*, Tetley's *Cask Bitter*, Timothy Taylor *Landlord*

Red Lion

570 Sheffield Road, S41 8LX. Telephone 01246 450770

Gaffer: Maureen Tropman

Smoking Throughout

Open: 12 to 11, 12 to 10.30 Sun

One rarely finds an Old Mill brewery pub and never further south than this great local at the edge of Chesterfield. The location is important because one might well stay in a nearby hotel, or arrive by passing the town and travelling into the ground along the Sheffield Road. I was really glad to put this into this years guide because it complements the nearby Derby Tup by offering an alternative that is patently also a friendly community pub.

Sometimes you know that the locals come to a pub because the company of the landlady is really comforting. I felt that it was a place where you might easily be mothered and cajoled into taking part in activities for the pub and as a consequence for charities. The main bar has numerous darts trophies and there is a big screen TV for those big matches Similarly Saturday night will find a pub-singer style of entertainment; quiz nights draw in others on quieter nights. The local CAMRA groups have promoted the pub for some time and the Old Mill guest beers are apparently the target for beer mat collectors. The seasonal ales are very popular. Don't expect to find lots of football fans going to the game. The locals are more likely to head north to Sheffield, shame on them. What you will find is a friendly pub with some real characters. It doesn't fit any stereotyped view of suburban local, nor real ale den. I really enjoyed my quiet lunch time pint and will certainly be back.

BWV 11.5.06: Old Mill *Bitter, Bullion, Mild*

Royal Oak

1 The Shambles S40 1PX. Telephone 01246 237700
Gaffers: Josh Clarke and Emma Randall
Food: Good value traditional English menu
11 to 4 Mon to Wed, 11 to 5 Thu to Sat
Separate smoking areas MP JB
Open: 11 to 7 Mon and Tue, 11 to 11 Wed to Sat, Closed Sun

MP JB

The sister, or perhaps daughter, pub of the Rutland is found in the historic Shambles area. This is the oldest pub in Chesterfield has recently been taken over by Ken of the Rutland and is run by his daughter, the expectation of good ale continues in a great location. A preservation order on the building helps to protect a remarkable non smoking Tudor bar complete with high timber-ramed, mediaeval-style ceilings and beautiful stained glass windows. The second bar is entered by a totally separate entrance and is on a lower level. Here the regulars find seats among tourists and business folk enjoying its rare quality under a lower ceiling with flag-stone floor. Expect good beers from the national chains of good quality, enough choice to satisfy most needs and friendly town centre locals and tourists to chat with.
UPDATE: It now has three regular plus three guest ales. The pub is essentially the same and more popular than last year.

BWV 24.3.05: Adnams *Broadside*, Badger *Tanglefoot*, Caledonian *Deuchars IPA*, Everards *Tiger*, Greene King *Abbot*, Stones *Bitter*
BWV 11.5.06: Bass *Draught*, Caledonian *Deuchars IPA*, Derby *Triple Hop*, Elgood's *Cambridge Bitter*, Greene King *Abbot*, Stones *Bitter*

Rutland Arms

23 Stephenson Place, S40 1XL Telephone 01246 205857
Gaffer: Ken Randall
Food: Good quality home cooked pub grub 12 to 7
Separate smoking areas
Open: 11 to 11 Sun to Wed, 11 to 12 Thu to Sat

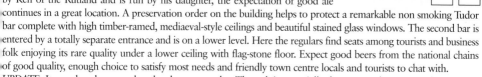

MP TV BM

Tracey recommended this pub as a '*not miss*' experience. She was right it is the best located and most interesting real ale pub in town. The interest comes in the form of 10 real ales at any one time, several served under gravity from directly behind the bar. The good location comes from being between the town bus stops and the crooked spire. The Rutland trades on its comfort, many regulars bring their paper for some peace and quite, other businessmen come for a real ale lunch and good value pub grub. The upshot is that we have here a good town ale house that offers something for everyone without the need for gimmicks.
UPDATE: The beer choice gets larger and the pub is as popular as ever.

BWV 24.3.05: Bateman *Spring Breeze*, Bath Ales *Gem*, Black Sheep *Bitter*, Boddingtons *Cask Bitter*, Caledonian *Deuchars IPA*, Everards *Original*. Greene King *Abbot, IPA*, Highgate *Natterjack*, Marston's *Pedigree*, Timothy Taylor *Landlord*
BMV 11.5.06 Adnams *Regatta*, Boddingtons *Cask Bitter*, Caledonian *Deuchars IPA*, Camerons *Castle Eden Ale*, Greene King *Abbot*, Hambleton *Nightmare Stout*, Harviestoun *Bitter and Twisted*, Hop Back *Odyssey*, Marston's *Pedigree*, Timothy Taylor *Landlord*, Tom Wood *Hop and Glory*, York *Decade*

Chesterfield

The Chesterfield skyline is dominated by that crooked spire, and the church at the bottom is large and interesting, for those interested in churches. The buildings around it should also be some of the most exclusive in Derbyshire, but they were utterly shabby: and the walk from the railway station to the town centre might make you feel like giving up. You will also be bewildered by lots of those stupid sign posts that every council in England seemed to buy in the 90s: the ones with ten pointers pointing to things nobody wants to go to, but without a pointer to the place you are desperate to find; and if it does have a useful pointer, someone will have climbed the pole after midnight and swiveled it! Having said all that though, there are parts of central Chesterfield that are quite nice.

Chesterfield Museum

This is a bright red brick building near the church. It is small, straightforward and concentrates, as it should, on the history of the town. Chesterfield has one of England's finest sets of markets in the grand central square. There is a covered market hall and a large open air market besides.

Saltergate

A medieval street name, with fine 18th Century terraces at the town end and a medieval style football ground at the other. The ground is worth visiting because it is one of the few left that has a pre war, if not pre historic, feel.

Crewe

The club was named after Princess Alexandra, who visited with her husband, the future King Edward VII, the year the club started. If they had used the Prince's name they would have been Crewe Albert. He changed names when he became King, but not his habits; so maybe they could have been Crewe Philanders.

Crewe was the first railway town, built in 1837 in the middle of one of England's richest and snootiest counties. You have to earn at least as much as a Premiership reserve striker to live comfortably in the rest of Cheshire, so Crewe is a bit inward looking. It is not unwelcoming, but most visitors come for the football and you can see the ground from the station; so why bother doing anything to point strangers to the town centre, let alone pretty towns near by?

Nantwich

This is a pretty old town. The name means 'famous salt works' A lot of the locals will not only know the Chief Constable of Cheshire, but also have his mobile number. Please do not scare them. Just because their dustbins are probably worth more than your house does not make them bad people. They just want to be left alone to enjoy complaining about the kinds of people they hardly ever see in real life; which is another thing they will hardly ever see.

Hack Green Secret Nuclear Bunker.

You never know when this will become a desirable property again. It is off the A530 out of Nantwich.
www.hackgreen.co.uk

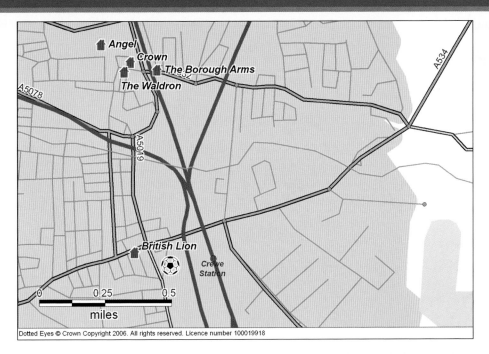

Angel
Crown
The Borough Arms
The Waldron
A5078
A5019
A534
British Lion
Crewe Station
0   0.25   0.5
miles

Dotted Eyes © Crown Copyright 2006. All rights reserved. Licence number 100019918

Angel

2 Victoria Centre, CW1 2PU. Telephone 01270 212003
Gaffer: John Hennessey
Food: Home-cooked English menu with specialities like mint pudding, steak pie and home made hot pot
Smoking Throughout
Open: 10 to 7 Mon to Fri, 10 to 10 Sun

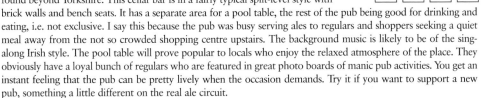

| MP | TV | BM | PG |

Another rarity for this guide is to recommend a pub located in a newish shopping precinct. Hidden downstairs is a new outlet for Oakwell ales, rarely found beyond Yorkshire. This cellar bar is in a fairly typical split-level style with brick walls and bench seats. It has a separate area for a pool table, the rest of the pub being good for drinking and eating, i.e. not exclusive. I say this because the pub was busy serving ales to regulars and shoppers seeking a quiet meal away from the not so crowded shopping centre upstairs. The background music is likely to be of the sing-along Irish style. The pool table will prove popular to locals who enjoy the relaxed atmosphere of the place. They obviously have a loyal bunch of regulars who are featured in great photo boards of manic pub activities. You get an instant feeling that the pub can be pretty lively when the occasion demands. Try it if you want to support a new pub, something a little different on the real ale circuit.
UPDATE: A big screen is now in place for those terrestrial big matches.

BWV 10.3.05 Oakwell *Barnsley Bitter, Barnsley Old Tom*
BWV 16.3.06: Oakwell *Barnsley Bitter, Acorn Lager, Oakwell Lager*

SP · TV · BM · PG · D

British Lion

58 Nantwich Road, CW2 6AL. Telephone 01270 254999
Gaffer: John Ruddock
Smoking Throughout
Open: 12 to 5, 7 to 11 Mon, 7 to 11 Tue to Thu, 12 to 11 Fri and Sat

Very occasionally you can find a decent ale pub close to the ground and the British Lion is one such example. You can expect the unexpected in terms of ales among the six a week on offer alongside the regular Tetley's. This recently redecorated single bar gets very busy on matchdays yet is welcoming to away fans who love their ales. Younger adults can find a space with parents in the rear of the pub leaving the regulars to chat beer and ale in the simple clean bar area. My lunchtime visit became a much longer session as we chatted over the merits of Dario's management and the fun I have always had when visiting Crewe. As with many pubs the number of ales increases at the weekend when the footie trade means larger demand. The British Lion is also very convenient for the station making it ideal for the last pint before going home.
UPDATE: Jed, the footie fan barman, has moved on but the friendliness remains. It is open earlier on match days and has plans for an outside area for those who wish to smoke. The beer list continues to change every few days and often includes a mild.

BWV 10.3.05: Harviestoun *Schiehallion*, Hampshire *Lionheart*, Tetley's *Cask Bitter*, *Dark Mild*
BWV 16.3.06: Black Sheep *Bitter*, Caledonian *Deuchars IPA*, Tetley's *Cask Bitter*

MP · SKY · BM

The Borough Arms

New

33 Earle Street, CW1 2BG. Telephone 01270 254999
Gaffer: John Webster
Separate smoking areas
Open: 7 to 11 Mon to Thu, 3 to 11 Fri, 12 to 4, 7 to 11 Sat, 12 to 3, 7 to 10.30 Sun

A breath of fresh air has blown into the Borough Arms and all is changing for the better. John has taken over and while continuing the brilliant beer policy he is also in the process of developing the massive potential of this renowned ale house. The plans are something very special and the entry of the Borough into the guide certainly shoots Crewe up the league table of real ale towns.

The pub was being redecorated when I visited but there is no intention to change the cosy nature of the place. It has small rooms off a central bar and a range of ales that Rachel, the bar supervisor, is quick to recommend. John, the Forest supporting landlord, has such enthusiasm and it was with great relish that he talked about opening the downstairs rooms so that the cellar and brewing plant could be seen by beer lovers as they tick away. My evening was spent with John, Henry, Kerry and Matt, talking about real ale, the Alex and how good the pub is. The quiz teams were due to arrive as I left; this is really a community local that will soon have a national reputation. Belgian ales are the next new offering to be found on the list The Never be Hinde is the first of the home pub brews, the name paying homage to the previous pub brewer.

BWV 16.3.06: Beartown *White Admiral*, Borough Arms Brewery *Never be Hinde*, Crouch Vale *Snow Drop*, O'Hanlon's *Firefly*, *Port Stout*, *Yellow Hammer*, Sarah Hughes *Dark Ruby*, Woodlands *Bitter*, *Midnight Stout*

Crown

25 Earle Street, CW1 2BH. Telephone 01270 257295
Gaffer: Maureen Aitken
Smoking Throughout
Open: 11 to 11 Sun to Thu, 11 to 12 Fri and Sat

Those real ale heads who seek out good pubs only to find a really grumpy brewer will often find heaven in the pub next door. This was my experience of the Crown where there was an instant welcome and an understanding of how footie fans like you and me help to make a pub what it is. This pub is spotless and has many quirky features that sell the love of good ale. The polished mirror tiles above the bar, the French railway prints, the frosted hotel windows; all suggest this is a place to cherish and protect through regular custom. This is my type of pub, even down to the crib aboard inviting you to enter into traditional pastimes while quaffing the quality Robinson's ales. As with most of their pubs the variety is such that there isn't a need to offer masses of guest ales. I really enjoyed my hour or so here and the barman was a mine of information on the rival real ale pubs. It has a traditional real ale clientele, generally being locals who know the value of a good friendly pub.
UPDATE: Plans include a conversion of a pleasant courtyard for alfresco drinking. The Crown remains as friendly as ever, a place to make new friends.

BWV 10.3.05: Robinson's *Enigma, Old Tom, Hatters Mild, Unicorn*
BWV 16.3.06: Robinson's *Enigma, Hatters Mild, Old Tom, Unicorn*

The Waldron **New**

Prince Albert Street, CW1 2DJ. Telephone 01270 254608
Gaffer: Simone Williams
Food: Good value, good quality pub grub 12 to 10
Separate smoking areas
Open: 11 to 11 Mon to Thu, 11 to 12 Fri and Sat, 12 to 10.30 Sun

The Waldron was the recommendation of locals who suggested that a new pub was trying to offer a real ale alternative to the many keg pubs in the town. Barracuda opened the pub in September 2005, converting the dole office into a spacious open plan tavern in the town centre big pub style. The conversion was extensive and includes televisions in every nook and cranny and also in the pub garden. They will be ahead of the game for the world cup games and you get a flavour of their intentions when you see the list of up and coming sports events. It has a good location, in an area undergoing regeneration and across the road from Earle Street. The younger ale drinkers will like the pub but it has also already encouraged an own older clientele, being busy with lunchtime office workers and late evening party animals. The beer selection will doubtless expand. It will take some time to convince the traditional ale heads but that is always the case with new developments. John, the duty manager, was keen to stress the family nature of the pub, the welcome you will get and the fact that it is always a fun place to work. The afternoon was developing into a serious Cheltenham watching session when I left for the next pub. I look forward to returning next year to see how great plans come to fruition.

BWV 16.3.05: Archers *Village*, Flowers *IPA*

COMPETITION WINNER

The winner of the competition was Malcolm Claringbold. His entry into the competition was made over a lunchtime session with Mally and his Carlisle supporting mates in the Inn on The Green in Bristol. As a condition of him getting a brown envelope stuffed with beer tokens I asked him to describe his football and real ale experiences and elaborate on his recommendations for best pubs. The description that follows will no doubt strike a chord with those of us who have similar histories of life in the lower leagues, with glories to be remembered for a life time.

My dad first took me to a game circa 1958/59 The sixties were relatively kind to CUFC, particularly at 'Fortress Brunton' and laid the foundation for our promotion to the old First division, those halcyon days when, oh so briefly, we topped the footballing world. Since then the club has indeed embarked on a rollercoaster ride to rival Alton Towers' Corkscrew. Surviving the Knighton days (ball-juggling chairmen, aliens et al), rescued by clubs going bust (before the days of administration and CVA's), a last gasp goal from an on loan keeper, two trips to Wembley, two to Cardiff and a season on loan to non-league oblivion, Actually the season in the conference was reasonably enjoyable but only because we escaped at the first time of asking. Add to that the Supporters' Trust taking the owner to the High Court, and is it any wonder BBC 5Live voted Carlisle the most exciting football club to follow over the last decade.

Last season after a few early setbacks it became very easy to follow Carlisle home and away. Most home games find me in the Rugby Club where they serve 2 regular beers, Yates and Theakston, and a guest. Amongst the away trips last year I particularly enjoyed our trip to The Crown in Stockport, most impressed by the 14 hand pumps and especially the fact that none of them was serving Robinson's despite the pressure from the brewery barons on the local council. Dave and I took our preparation seriously when we visited Bristol and arranged to meet up with Stedders in The Inn on the Green before our visit to the Memorial Ground. The Cemetery in Rochdale should be included on the itinerary for all visiting fans, well worth the extra couple of minutes walk from the ground. We were lucky when visiting Mansfield that it coincided with St George's weekend celebrations and a beer festival at The Bold Forester where the landlord not only took a pride in his beers but seemed pleased to share his enthusiasm with fellow topers. Another favourite, as recommended for inclusion in the guide was the Railway View in Macclesfield, only 10 minutes from the ground, 'beers well kept and good craic.'

The results of the competition are published on the website. There will be another one next year and anyone can win. I hope Mally enjoys the beers he might well buy his mates over the year. It is just a shame that our teams are parting company. If you visit the Carlisle Rugby club please say hello to him for me, I know you will have a good time in what is the best place to drink before a game when visiting Brunton Park.

Mally and his mates, in the Kings Head, Carlisle, celebrating his win as England thrash Sweden (not)

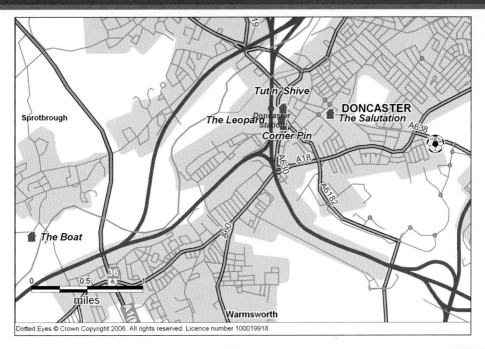

Sprotbrough

Tut'n' Shive

The Leopard

Doncaster Station

Corner Pin

DONCASTER
The Salutation

A638

A18

A630

A60

A6182

The Boat

36

0   0.5   1
miles

Warmsworth

A1(M)

A19

The Boat

Nursery Lane, DN5 7NB. Telephone 01302 858500 **New**

Gaffer: Paul Trigg

Food: Good value traditional menu, all chef-prepared. 12 to 10 Mon to Sat, 12 to 9.30 Sun

Separate smoking areas

Open: 10 to 11, 10 to 10.30 Sun

F

CP | BM | D

I know that many of you like to go for a meal in a country pub, often nowhere near the town you will be visiting. The Boat has been one of my regular stopping off points over the last ten years; I often drop in here when travelling up the A1 and want a break for good food in a old fashioned country pub. This is definitely not a football pub. It is the now classic food pub that also does good real ale. Bring your girlfriend not your mates, meet with friends who have come from far flung places and catch up over a good pub meal. Best of all, stretch your legs with a stroll along the nearby River Don and then find one of the many corners of this stone walled farmhouse for a pint of best.

At all times the pub has a good mix of walkers, cyclists, business men and couples all settling for food and ale. The pub has several different internal rooms, all with feature fire places and windows. Given the name of the pub it is somewhat of a surprise, therefore, that there is no direct to the river side. It does have an excellent outside courtyard with masses of benches and covers that are evidence of its popularity on warm summer evenings. This garden is enclosed by the pub, another farm building and a stable block. The pub looks historic; it has been an ale house since 1642 but only in its present form since 1985. It is a classic of its type.

BWV 12.5.06: Black Sheep *Bitter*, John Smith's *Cask Bitter*

Corner Pin

145 St. Sepulcher Gate, DN1 3AH. Telephone 01302 323159
Gaffer: Howard Rimmer
Smoking Throughout
Open: 12 to 11.30

This is the ultimate in street-corner pubs. I visited as the smell of repainting was still in the air and I quickly felt that I had found the true gem in the Doncaster scene. The room literally wraps itself around the bar, darts at one end, lounge at the other. The central section is intimate as the drinkers sit at benches with only a table and chair between them and the bar. Evidence of an even smaller past is found in the windows, the glass portraying the tap and smoke rooms. My lunchtime visit found visitors from a nearby training course, complete with name tags and liquid lunch. I was also able to compare notes of real ale pubs with '*Moaning Steve*', his list being of railway related ale chasing; there were remarkable similarities and differences. This is my favourite in Donny. The place will maybe get even better as Moaning Steve says it '*offers an excellent choice of well kept ales.*'
UPDATE: CAMRA Pub of the season for Spring 2006 says it all.

BWV 16.3.05: Fuller's **London Pride**, John Smith's **Cask**, Theakston's **Bitter**, Wells **Bombardier**
BWV 12.5.06: Kelham Island **Easy Rider**, John Smith's **Cask Bitter**, Wold Top **Falling Stone**, Mars **Magic**

The Leopard

1 West Street, DN1 3AA. Telephone 01302 363054
Gaffer: Alan McHugh
Separate smoking areas
Open: 11 to 11

There have been many times over the last year when I have been contacted by friends, stranded at Doncaster Station on their way home from a game, who have said the Leopard is a great pub. I visited this year and found this to be so true. It offered, an ale that I have never seen before, an atmosphere that is fast being lost to trendy plasticisation, and to top it all, a list of gigs to attract the now-aging music fan. The pub has two large rooms, both with high ceilings and no concessions to modern décor. The bar has a pool table, while the lounge is split into two areas, one of which is non-smoking. The room upstairs holds 200 or so when Wilco Johnson or Bad Manners call in to play. This pub is famous as a launch pad for up and coming artists, Keane and Travis have made recent appearances. The reassuring statement re music is that Karaoke will never be part of the scene, it is talent, and loads of it, even in the Sunday afternoon jam sessions. The regulars are very mixed in both age and attitude. The students are likely to mix well with the good old boys who have drunk here all their life. There are plans to make the West Street area into the Bohemian Quarter. Alan has seen the pub and the area change since 1992. The pub gets better and the local area will doubtless benefit from some gentrification, but Bohemian? Will it be poetry workshops next?

BWV 12.5.06: Caledonian **Deuchars IPA**, Glentworth **Kiwi King**, John Smith's **Cask Bitter**, Theakston's **Best Bitter**

The Salutation

14 South Parade, DN1 2DR. Telephone 01302 340705
Gaffer: Jon Ferguson
Food: Good quality traditional pub food 12 to 3, 6 to 9 Mon to Sat,
12 to 6 Sun
Separate smoking areas
Open: 12 to 11, 12 to 10.30 Sun

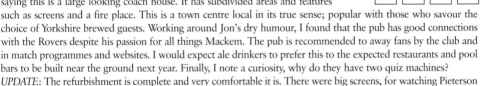

As if to fit the theme of change I managed to meet Jon at the Salutation just before it underwent a refurbishment. I will therefore, save the description to saying this is a large looking coach house. It has subdivided areas and features such as screens and a fire place. This is a town centre local in its true sense; popular with those who savour the choice of Yorkshire brewed guests. Working around Jon's dry humour, I found that the pub has good connections with the Rovers despite his passion for all things Mackem. The pub is recommended to away fans by the club and in match programmes and websites. I would expect ale drinkers to prefer this to the expected restaurants and pool bars to be built near the ground next year. Finally, I note a curiosity, why do they have two quiz machines?
UPDATE: The refurbishment is complete and very comfortable it is. There were big screens, for watching Pieterson in action when I visited. The beer garden is likely to be changed next. They now have six guest ales.

BWV 16.3.05: Everards *Original*, North Yorkshire *Best*, Robinson's *Champion*, Springhead *The Leveller*, Tetley's *Cask Bitter*
BWV 12.5.06: Acorn *White Oak*, Cairngorm *Sheepshagger*, Greene King *Abbot*, North Yorkshire *Dizzy Blonde*, *Flying Herbert*, Shepherd Neame *Kent's Best*, Tetley's *Cask Bitter*

Tut n' Shive

6 West Laithe Gate, DN1 1SF. Telephone 01302 360300
Gaffer: Nick Coster
Food: Good value traditional pub food 12 to 6 Mon to Sat, 12 to 5 Sun
Smoking Throughout
Open: 11 to 11 Mon to Thu, 11 to 12 Fri and Sat, 12 to 12 Sun

This pub is new to the Greene King stable and as such the beers here are likely to change but remain genuine real ales with guests. Being very close to the station, it gets very busy, as it is the obvious choice as you enter the shopping area. It is worthy of its popularity because the welcome is good and the clientele pretty relaxed. It is dark; dark walls, wooden ceilings and stone floors; in fact the bar stands out as illumination in the created and intentional gloom. It is in the style of so many ale houses in the 90s looking slightly worn by design. You can practice traditional pub pastimes like spot the beer map on the walls, or name the tune on the rocking juke box. As it says '*the ales are noted, are quoted, are voted the best.*' The students in the day relish cheap grub, the townies in the evening live here for the youthful atmosphere. In all it is a really good town boozer with space to either chat or party.
UPDATE: The pub was as busy as ever and this is apparently always the norm here.

BWV 16.3.05: Black Sheep *Bitter*, Boddingtons *Cask Bitter* Everards *Original*, Greene King *IPA*, *Abbot*, Springhead *Roaring Meg*
BWV 12.5.06: Black Sheep *Bitter*, Greene King *Abbot*, *IPA*, *Old Speckled Hen*, *Prospect*, Timothy Taylor *Landlord*

Doncaster

A town with a long history. You can visit, walk down some central streets and think it is rich and smart: but if you walk down the wrong roads it can seem a complete closet of a place. The worst part of Doncaster was always the stinking subway outside the railway station and the grotty, rough holed end of a shopping centre at the end of it.

Doncaster Museum

Doncaster's website only tells you about one thing, a gallery called 'By River and Road', which '…tells the story of Doncaster and its region through the twin routes of the River Don and the Great North Road in an exciting and innovative way.' So Doncaster has given up on having a museum and decided to have a narrative thread instead, but cannot be bothered to tell you what you will actually see if you go inside.

The Museum of the King's Own Yorkshire Light Infantry is in the same building but you have to stumble around Doncaster's website to find that out. It seems to have avoided pillage and destruction by interactive barbarians and multi-heritage harpies, but cannot be long for this world of liberal extreme intolerance.

Belle View

We are not sure what of beauty you were supposed to be viewing from this ground. The grandstand of the racecourse next door that is higher than the football ground is wide? Or maybe the car park that looks like an Action Man sized diorama of the Somme Battlefield?

Gillingham

The least interesting of the Medway towns; Rochester is historic, with a castle and cathedral; Chatham was important, with the Royal Dockyard; and Gillingham was where the workers lived. All of them suffered economic problems when the Dockyard closed. London's closeness drives up the cost of housing and food, and important things like beer. Strangers leaving Gillingham station saw a grotty street full of boarded up shops. Most left without discovering that it is the High Street!

The most 'famous' Gillinghamite was Will Adam, who founded the modern Japanese navy. So if Gillingham had been less boring he may have stayed, and Pearl Harbour may never have happened.

Chatham Historic Dockyard

HMS Victory was built here, but unfortunately for Medway's tourist industry it ended up in Portsmouth. The Medway was the scene of perhaps Europe's greatest naval triumph when in 1697 the Dutch Navy sailed in and took, or burnt, most of the Royal Navy's ships. The Dutch could do this because the English Parliament gave Charles II no money to pay for sailor's wages, so there weren't any. There's a lot in this Museum, but it is expensive.

Charles Dickens

Dickens' family moved here from Portsmouth when he was five, and he died here in 1870. There are more things with plaques on in this town than you will find in a Glasgow dentist's waiting room; so you can discover which buildings he wrote about without reading his books.
www.medwaytowns.com

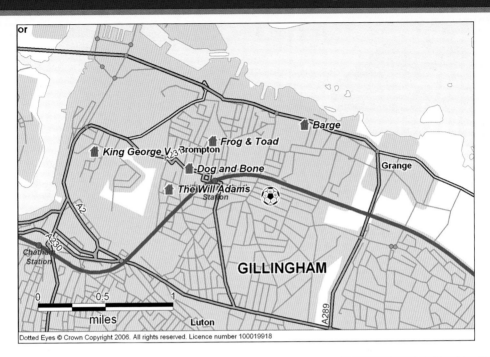

Dotted Eyes © Crown Copyright 2006. All rights reserved. Licence number 100019918

Barge

63 Layfield Road, ME7 2QY. Telephone 01634 850485
Gaffer: Tim Robinson
Smoking Throughout
Open: 7 to 11 Mon to Thu, 4 to 11 Fri, 12 to 11 Sat and Sun

This is a beautiful street-terrace pub. Not in the oldie worldy sense that, because of the views out of the dimply lit bar to the Medway valley beyond the garden and the simple comfort of a timber framed ship lap style Kent Cottage pub, *'It blows the cobwebs away'* (Mark Morgan of Burnley) When you visit there will often be an odd guitar around and the locals are known to pick one up and set off an impromptu folk singing session. The list of upcoming events is impressive, including acts of world renown. In the CAMRA guide for 14 years, the Barge serves Cottage ales as a staple, with four others rotating every few days. The pub proclaims *'there are no strangers here, only friends who have not met'*. The family atmosphere oozes from the woodwork. It is a top boozer, my advice is to park up nearer the ground and walk down for a friendly lunchtime pint.

UPDATE: The Barge continues to be a favourite to those who manage to find it. Nelson beers are not likely to be here any more.

BWV 6.4.05: Bass *Draught*, Cottage *Leg before Whippet*, Flagship *Spring Pride*, Nelson *Joshua Ale*, Wells *Eagle*
BWV 21.5.06: Cottage *Champflower Ale*, *Golden Arrow*, Daleside *Shrimpers*, Skinner's *Spriggers Ale*, Young's *Bitter*

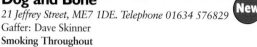

Dog and Bone

21 Jeffrey Street, ME7 1DE. Telephone 01634 576829
Gaffer: Dave Skinner
Smoking Throughout
Open: 11 to 11 Mon to Sat, 12 to 10.30 Sun

The Dog and Bone has long been popular with both home and away fans looking for a convenient pub in the town centre that is large enough for groups to mix well before a game. It has been recommended to me by fans who prefer their pub to be in the town and handy for a short walk to or from the station

    The pub has undergone fairly recent extension to create a large eating area through a conservatory that extends away from the older part of the pub. The rest of the pub consists of a traditional two section layout with low timbered ceilings in the bar and lounge style. Dave has been landlord here for many years and knows the local pub scene. The locals are typical of the town centre and they are made up of a good mix of ages and attitudes. At lunch time it will be shoppers and office workers, in the evenings the local regulars enjoy a friendly and lively atmosphere. On matchdays there will be both home and away fans, often in separate areas of the pub but more likely sharing the love of the game in their conversation. I chatted with David Green, a local accountant, who told me that he was one of many who travel longer distances to enjoy the atmosphere and beer selections at the Dog and Bone. The beers are often changing and include a mix of national and regional ales.

BWV 21.5.06: Eccleshall *Slaters Original*, Greene King *IPA*, Vale *Edgar's Golden Ale*

Frog & Toad

Burnt Oak Terrace, ME7 1DR. Telephone 01634 852231
www.thefrogandtoad.com
Gaffer: David Gould
Food: Traditional good value pub food
Bookings only on Sunday 5 to 7 Mon to Thu, 1 to 4 Sun
Smoking Throughout
Open: 11 to 11, 12 to 10.30 Sun

The Frog and Toad was local CAMRA pub of the year three years running. It is a very quirky place to drink, a true residential town pub and the hub of local life. It runs 4 darts teams, 2 quiz teams, 2 footie teams yet is not a true footie pub in the big screen definition. The oddities are legendary. For examples the basket in the ceiling is for hoisting the shoes of those who wish to partake of Kwak Beer and gallows in the beer garden, heaven knows why this is of use. David also has 30 Belgian beers on offer and is truly led by the locals' wishes in the choice of ales and activities. The place comes to life as the office trade come in for cheap food after work, Monday to Thursday. This is a fun pub without the need for town centre themes; I would love it as my local.

UPDATE: David is the new Guvn'or, having previously been manager here for the last six years. The fun will continue as will the frequent themed festivals. The next was of *'beers with place names.'* The Belgian beer festival is now a May fixture.

BWV 6.4.05: Brakspear *Bitter*, Fuller's *London Pride*, Marston's *Pedigree*. Skinner's *Best*, Biddenden *Bushels Cider*
BWV 21.5.06: Brakspear *Bitter*, Fuller's *London Pride*, Harveys *Sussex Mild*, Robinson's *Unicorn*

King George V

1 Prospect Row, Brompton, ME7 5AL. Telephone 01634 842418
www.kgvpub.com
Gaffer: John Brice
Food: Big menu from simple to exotic and elaborate food
12 to 2, 6.30 to 8.30 Tue to Sat, 12 to 4 Sun
Separate smoking areas
Open: 11.45 to 11 Mon to Sat, 12 to 10.30 Sun

John certainly knows a good beer and the KGV is a great place to spend an hour
or so before the 35 minute walk to the ground. This street-corner pub has
reinvented itself as a local's pub that serves the local community needs. They also specialise in malt whiskies, Belgian
bottles ales and treat their customers as officers, whatever their rank. The bar is a curious shape, like the prow of
a galleon with the bars wrapping themselves cosily around the corners of the building. Local history and character
is evident on every wall. For example, a print of the pub pre-stoning, known then as the King of Prussia, and
military badges and plaques. It too has themed beer evenings but every day the choice of ales always includes a
range of gravities and often a mild.
UPDATE: Dave, the Torquay supporting Landlord, is planning to open the improved pub garden and convert
rooms for bed and breakfast accommodation. The train to Gillingham is really only five minutes away in Chatham.

BWV 6.4.05: Adnams *Best*, Brakspear *Bitter*, Greene King *Old Speckled Hen*, Goacher's *Light*
BWV 21.5.06: Adnams *Bitter*, Smiles *Bitter*, St. Peter's *Mild*

The Will Adams

73 Saxton Street, ME7 5EG. Telephone 01634 575902 **New**
Gaffer: Peter Lodge
Food: Football menu when Gills are at home 12 to 2
Smoking Throughout
Open: 7 to 11 Mon to Fri, 12 to 5, 7 to 11 Sat and Sun.
Earlier opening on matchdays

The Will Adams is one of those pubs that just has to be seen and sampled. It is
a local award winner and comes highly recommended by many of the readers
of last years' guides who said it was essential visiting for football fans who love
a quality real ale pub that is run by a proper football enthusiast.
    Peter is a season ticket holder and a lot of what the pub does has connections to his love of ale, proper pub life
and football. The ales always include Summer Lightning and three others that are constantly changing. He also
specialises in thirty plus malt whiskies and a real cider. You will always be welcome as an away fan because Peter
has enjoyed, (or is it suffered?) the experiences of finding good ale on his away days following the Gills. There is a
photo in the bar of Peter and fellow pub drinkers at the Withdean, a connection that is long established when the
Seagulls decamped to Priestfield all those years ago. The whole length of one room has a mural that depicts the day
that Will Adams left for Japan and his Samurai existence. This theme continues on through amusing pictures on
the toilet doors. The pub is board game and darts mad. An odd variation is the Kentish dart board and the pub
team that plays in the local league. The age of the regular's ranges from the mid twenties, to Charlie, who is in his
eighties, all are friendly folk as is the landlord and his good lady. This is a great back-street pub with real ale class.

BWV 21.5.06: Hop Back *Summer Lightning*, Hydes *Jekyll's Gold*, St. Austell *Tribune*, York *Decade*

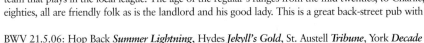

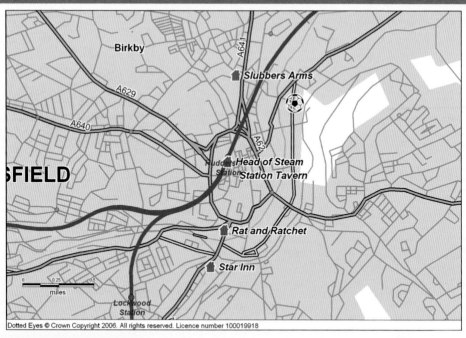

Birkby

A641

Slubbers Arms

A629

A640

A62

SFIELD

Huddersfield Station

Head of Steam

Station Tavern

Rat and Ratchet

Star Inn

0   0.25   0.5

miles

Lockwood Station

MP | TV | BM | D

Head of Steam

St Georges Square, HD1 1JB. Telephone 01484 454533 **New**
Gaffer: David Mansfield
**Food: Wide range of locally sourced home cooked food 11.30 to 9,
11.30 to 5 Sat, 12 to 7 Sun
Separate smoking areas
Open: 11 to 12.30 Mon to Thu, 11 to 2 Sat, 12 to 10.30 Sun**

At the other end of the Station platform is the Head of Steam, a pub chain that has a great real ale reputation, and, in the case of the Huddersfield version, great buildings in which to enjoy the ale and rail kick.

The rooms in this pub are stunningly grand. Each has unique character. The rear houses a fantastic set of Live Aid photographs that are for sale from the Landlord and also has access to the platform, should you be waiting for a train. I frequented the locals' room that had impressive collections of railway memorabilia and curiously, toy vehicles. It really is a bit of a sweet shop if you want to sample good ales in a distinctive location. Those locals and not so local regulars will include the inevitable rail and beer tickers. It is also very useful for those heading off to Leeds for the night as there is ample room for groups of all sizes to meet. On matchdays there is likely to be restrictions on entry, enforced by the local constabulary and door persons. Come here without colours and you will meet some great local people, the sort who make the drinking of real ale the benefit for football fans who enjoy mixing with the locals. Blues and jazz gigs are held on Monday and Wednesday evenings. For me it was on to a similar bar in Dewsbury that made for a great evening train-driven session.

BWV 2.3.06: Archers *Admiral Lord Rooney*, Bradfield *Brown Cow*, Black Sheep *Bitter*, Brakspear *Bitter*, Highgate *Dark Mild*, Holt *Bitter*, Weston's *Old Rosie*

Rat and Ratchet

40 Chapel Hill, HD1 3EB. Telephone 01484 542400
Gaffer: David Kendall-Smith
Food: Good value traditional pub food 12 to 2 Wed to Sat
Separate smoking areas
Open: 3 to 12 Mon and Tue, 12 to 12 Wed and Thu,
12 to 11.30 Fri and Sat, 12 to 11 Sun

CP | TV | JB | PG

The facade of the Rat and Ratchet suggests a town boozer, the interior a country farmhouse. The range of beers is large and the quality I sampled particularly good. Each level and nook of the pub has a distinctive character as it rambles away from the main road. For me I enjoyed the selection of music posters from the 60s and beyond, especially the Bob Marley photo near the toilets. Go on have a go at an Ossett fest, the full range is available and just asks to be sampled. You might have to compete for the leather sofas, forget them, get to the bar and get into a chat about the Terriers, Yorkshire cricket or rugby league, not necessarily in that order.
UPDATE: David has refitted the garden and a new bar will soon follow. It may have a younger feel.

BWV 13.3.05: Copper Dragon *Black Gold*, Jarrow *Palmers Resolution*, Mordue *Millennium Bridge*, Ossett *Excelsior*, *March Hare*, *Pale Gold*, *R+R*, *Silver King*, Slaters *Original*, Timothy Taylor *Landlord*, *Best*, Weston's *Old Rosie Cider*
BWV 2.3.06: Leatherbritches *Goldings*, Mighty Oak *Indian Pale Ale*, *Oscar Wilde*, Newby Wyke *England Expects*, Kingston *Topaz*, Ossett *Excelsior*, *Pale Gold*, *Silver King*, Pictish *Brewers Gold*, Timothy Taylor *Best*, *Landlord*, Farmers *Tipple Cider*

Slubbers Arms

1 Halifax Old Road, Hillhouse, HD1 6HW. Telephone 01484 429032 **New**
Gaffer: Mike Parrish
Food: Pie and peas on matchdays, new home cooked menu on other days
12 to 2
Separate smoking areas
Open: 12 to 2.30, 5.30 to 11.30 Mon to Sat, 12 to 3, 7 to 11.30 Sun

F

SP

The Slubbers is a Timothy Taylor house on the main Bradford Road, about ten mins walk from the ground and with ample street parking nearby. That is far too simple a description of this wonderful triangular street corner local. It is the characters and the Landlord that make this pub so special. Mike and the locals have made this a bit of a football institution. He arrived relatively recently but has continued the tradition of welcoming all to this pub and encouraging the traditions of good old Yorkshire honesty when discussing ale and football, or in his case, rugby league.
The pub consists of three quirky little rooms, the best being the flag-stoned tap room at the apex of the triangle. Scarves from clubs hang from an airing frame in the second room. This too was where the business people were found enjoying a late liquid lunch. I became engrossed in a conversation with Mike at the bar, that chat being enlightening to me as to the future of the pub business and the joys of this pub. I would have loved to have met the two Bob's, 'Wobbly' and 'Body Builder.' I had to move on before those regulars came in to test the next guest ale or two. The Slubbers name is related to the removal of knots from wool and silk. Not much has changed here since the loos were enclosed in 1992, the planned redecoration should only add to the character of this fantastic friendly pub.

BWV 2.3.06: Empire *Longshanks*, Timothy Taylor *Best*, *Golden Best*, *Landlord*

Star Inn

7 Albert Street, Lockwood, HD1 3PJ. Telephone 01484 545443
www.thestarinn.info
Gaffer: Sam Watt
Smoking Throughout
Closed Mon, Open 5 to 11 Tue to Fri, 12 to 11 Sat, 12 to 10.30 Sun

Sam's pub is more than a refurbishment, it is a four year old rebuild, but you would never know by the style of the place. I arrived on the Sunday of the beer festival where 40 plus ales had been reduced to just 8 or so. The marquee in the back yard still attracted the regulars who had made it such a success. There is purposely no music and the design encourages conversation throughout the house. The conversation, often ale related, is what makes the ambience so good. It holds numerous CAMRA awards and serves 15 to 20 different ales a week six guests at any one time to its unusual regular list. The Hydes poster claims *'Everyone likes a quick one'*. Nonsense, this is a place to savour at your leisure, a top boozer with top quality management that makes the place something special.

UPDATE: Check the website for details of the March, July and December festivals.

BWV 13.3.05: Archers *Spring Blond*, Brunswick *Pilsener*, Cottage *Jack's Bitter*, Copper Dragon *Black Gold*, E+S *Best*, *Empire Strikes Back*, Leyden *Referee*, Pictish *Brewers Gold*, Timothy Taylor *Best*, *Landlord*
BWV 2.3.06: Archers *Pie Eater*, Cottage *Between the Posts*, Goose Eye *Over and Stout*, Halifax *Possibly Organic*, *Jamaican Ginger*, Pictish *Brewers Gold*, Purity *Pure UBU*, Timothy Taylor *Landlord*

Station Tavern

St. Georges Square, HD1 1JB. Telephone 01484 511058
Gaffers: Bruce Travis and Michelle Pursell
Food: Sandwiches now available
Smoking Throughout
Open: 11.30 to 11, 12 to 10.30 Sun

So often a station-related pub is full of railwayiana, not this Tavern. It is just as the waiting room would have been. It has large, open fires, high ceilings and a window on to the platform for checking arrival times. It is like a church village hall complete with stone walls, stained glass windows and a reverential echo on first arrival. Bruce discovered the gorgeous floor tiling under the carpets, and they make a fine sight. It is the beer; however, that makes the popularity of the Station Tavern. Rarer Yorkshire beers including a mild, plus quality that is guaranteed, plus great Yorkshire humour; all make this the perfect starting or finishing point to Huddersfield's real ale scene. Harold would no doubt approve of this pub in the square that is the birthplace of rugby league. (George Hotel opposite) My visit found locals getting a quick pint or two before the St. Patrick's Day parade leading to a quicker than usual departure. A year later it seemed the same locals were still drinking here and the welcome was equally friendly.

UPDATE: Music is now on a Wednesday evening, nothing has changed.

BWV 13.3.05: Daleside *Blonde*, Golcar *Dark Mild*, Goose Eye *Golden Goose*, Newby Wyke *Grantham Gold*, Timothy Taylor *Landlord*, Wold Top *Bitter*, Yorkshire COTY
BWV 2.1.06: Bradfield *Farmers Stout*, Dark Star *Old Ale*, *Empire Strikes Back*, Holme Valley *Old Forge Bitter*, Salamander *Bandana*, Timothy Taylor *Landlord*

Huddersfield

For a small town with much bigger neighbours, Huddersfield has achieved much. It may lack self important visitor attractions but has maintained standards in its museums and libraries; while too many other northern towns treat these as worth less than even lip service.

Railway Station and George's Square.

The station front is like a film set fasciae, covering something four times wider than it is deep, but it is still one of our best station frontages. The Square it faces is worth a look. One of the hotels is famous for being the birthplace of rugby league, or at least it would be if only more people were bothered about the game played by lions and led by donkeys. There is also a new statue of Harold, I managed to put some pounds in my pocket, Wilson, which stands on the ground; either to help with the myth of him being a common man who might have shuffled to catch a train rather than been chauffeur driven; or it might just be because his birthplace would not spring for a plinth.

The main museum in Huddersfield is the Tolson; which has good stuff like tractors. The art gallery and central library are housed in a fine 1930s building just down from the Town Hall. The town has a contemporary music festival and the gallery tries to match it; so both have the usual pot luck as to whether you get something that inspires inspiration, loathing or boredom.

Leyton Orient

Although London is England's richest city, by a big wedge, it has never dominated English football, until now. Nearly a third of the clubs in the Premiership are London clubs (over a third if you count Manchester United), so you have got to feel sorry for unsuccessful London clubs, and Orient has been more unsuccessful than most

'Wiv a ladder and some glasses.
You could see to Ackney Marshes.
If it wasn't for the 'Ouses in between.'
From: If it wasn't for the Ouses in between, *Bateman & Le Brunn, 1894.*

Hackney Marshes

Readers who know about football before the 'Year Zero' of the Premiership will know of Hackney Marshes. It was famous for having over a hundred football pitches squeezed so tightly together there was barely room for fat managers of pub teams to squeeze between them and shout at players only slightly less fat, being violently ill after failing to prove they could still drink 18 pints of flat beer and show these youngsters a thing or two! This is the real root of football, not some show biz circus grown fat on a satanic spill of media money: but even the Marshes may go the way of terraces and rattles. There are only 88 pitches left and a lot of them will become a car park for the Olympics. It is promised they will be restored to sport. It was promised Wembley would be finished on time. It was promised there would be less red tape and taxes.

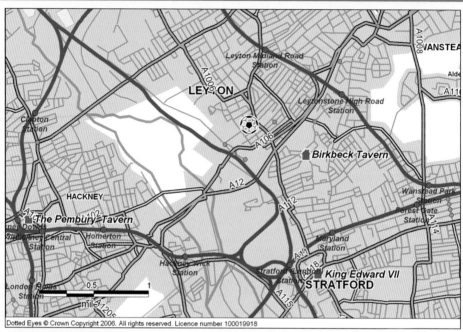

Dotted Eyes © Crown Copyright 2006. All rights reserved. Licence number 100019918

CP · TV · JB · PG · D

Birkbeck Tavern

45 Langthorne Road, Leytonstone, E11 4HL. Telephone 020 8539 2584
Gaffer: Kathy Wilson
Food: Various rolls
Smoking Throughout
Open: 11 to 11 Mon to Thu, 11 to 12 Fri and Sat, 12 to 11 Sun

The Birkbeck Tavern is the grand daddy of London lower division pubs. Any supporters of larger teams on a weekend away should make a tour to find this pub Kathy, the new landlady, has been here for many years and will doubtless continue the tradition of welcoming away fans. The pub operates a genuine two day maximum to turn round to new ale. It is popular with the '*Pigs Ear*' real ale crew and away fans who often phone in advance to check out the brews on offer. They are often surprised but rarely disappointed; over 300 different beers a year have been on offer. As one of my favourite haunts before a game, it is something very special. The atmosphere on matchdays is just perfect, totally friendly, especially on balmy summer's days when the garden comes into its own. In the middle of winter the genuine Leyton warmth comes to warm the cockles.
UPDATE: Roy has left for a well earned retirement and Kathy has taken up the reins. Live music on a Saturday is the only possible innovation to this great London local. The pub continues to shine.

BWV 25.1.05: Barnsley *Oakwell Bitter*, Rita's *Special (House Brew)*, St. Austell *Tinners*, Skinner's *Betty Stogs*
BWV 12.4.06: Archers *Spring Blonde*, Rita's *Special (House Brew)*, Welton's *Old Cocky*, *Randy Rabbit*

King Edward VII

47 Broadway, Stratford, E15 4BQ. Telephone 020 8534 2313 **New**

www.kingeddie.co.uk

Gaffer: Kendall Cordes

Food: Freshly prepared, home-cooked British menu 12 to 2.30, 6.30 to 10 Mon to Fri, 6.30 to 10 Sat, 12 to 9 Sun. Bar food 12 to 10 every day

Separate smoking areas

Open: 12 to 11 Mon to Wed, 12 to 12 Thu to Sat, 12 to 11.30 Sun

'*King Eddies*' has something of a legendary status in the East London real ale scene. It was great to visit it at last and find that all the rave reviews were indeed correct. It has historic value, great national ales, a policy that changes those beers regularly and good value and good quality food; all this and a great town centre location..

Kendall, the landlord, has an infectious enthusiasm for real ale and the potential of this pub. The historic value has to be mentioned. The best entrance is made via the tiled passageway into a fantastically traditional front bar. This room is the focal point for regular meetings of couples, business groups and shoppers from the mall opposite. The rear lounge has leather seats and is better suited for romantic liaisons. Then, at the back of the pub, is a raised area that has been extended to accommodate the restaurant. The locals are typical of the new Stratford, more affluent than in the past, definitely more likely to work in the city than in the docks. The clientele is as transient as the area that surrounds it. The pub is just as convenient for hammers fans but my choice would be to sit in the bar and watch London life walking past, safe in the knowledge that the train or bus will get you to Leyton a lot quicker than any car that crawls along the Broadway. This is a top pub and well worth the visit.

BWV 12.4.06: Adnams *Broadside*, Greene King *Old Speckled Hen*, Timothy Taylor *Landlord*, Wells *Bombardier*

The Pembury Tavern

90 Amhurst Road, Hackney, E8 1JH. Telephone 020 8986 8597 **New**

www.individualpubs.co.uk

Gaffer: Stephen Early

Street smoking

Open: 12 to 11

The Pembury is the third of the '*individual*' pubs in the guides and its opening has been anticipated ever since it was announced that this renovation would open again and serve a range of Milton ales, supplemented by micro-brew guests. It certainly meets my idea of what to do with a building that was facing apartment oblivion. The new flats surround the pub but the ale still flows and for once the community now has an improved facility. The pub was opened in Jan 2006 as a non-smoking modern-style pub with all the features of a traditional street local. This includes a bar billiards table, space that can be converted for local groups to meet, comfortable seating and room for the larger groups to congregate around the bar. It is essentially a wooden-floored, open-plan bar with that attractive echo of constant chatter that increases to a rumble of conversation as the day moves on. There is no music to distract the drinker, no obvious reasons for the real ale fan to look elsewhere in a hurry. I liked the simplicity, the Milton ales and the fact that there are two mainline stations within easy walking distance.

Any new pub deserves your custom, especially when it is bucking the nitro keg trend. Having survived a fire, being a biker's pub, trees growing through the roof and being a boxing venue, the building has lived a fantastically diverse life. It has now been given a great rebirth.

BWV 12.4.06: Butcombe *Bitter*, Milton *Daedalus, Minotaur, Pegasus, Sparta, Uluru*, Woodforde's *Great Eastern Ale*, Ben Crosman's *Prime Farmhouse Cider*

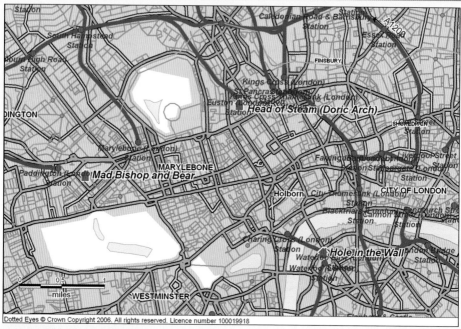

Dotted Eyes © Crown Copyright 2006. All rights reserved. Licence number 100019918

Head of Steam (Doric Arch) Euston Station

1 Eversholt Street, Euston, NW1 1DN. Telephone 020 7383 3359
www.theheadofsteam.co.uk
Gaffer: Dave O'Sullivan
Food: New menu, quality pub food 12 to 2.30, 5 to 9, 12 to 5 Sat
Separate smoking areas
Open: 11 to 11, 12 to 6 Sun

A station pub as they used to be? No, not cold and draughty, but with railway signs, carriage seating, friendly, helpful staff and a feeling that it's OK to miss the train because who wants to rush anyway. The Head of Steam name is spreading but this version still leads the way in creating a real ale club virtually on the station concourse. There are usually up to nine ever-changing real ales. When planning my journeys home it has always been a place to factor in to travel times, i.e. wherever you are leave time for the HoS before getting the train from Euston. It has one large bar that is creatively split into separate areas and levels. The TVs are very discrete I particularly like to find space in what looks like a mini-railway carriage complete with no smoking signs and bench seats so close to each other you can read the paper of your fellow commuter.

UPDATE: Fullers have taken it into their fold but guests continue. A refurbishment of the frontage may include the new name but only plasma screens and furnishings will add a touch of modernism.

BWV 6.12.04: Banks's *Original*, Black Sheep *Bitter*, Caledonian *Santa's Little Helper*, Dark Star *Porter*, *Special Edition*, Weston's *Vintage Cider*
BWV 1.11.05: Archers *Village*, Cottage *Western Glory*, Fuller's *Discovery*, *ESB*, London *Pride*, *Trafalgar*, Hopback *GFB*, Phoenix *White Tornado*, Weston's *Old Rosie*, *Vintage Ciders*

Hole in the Wall

5 Mepham Street, Waterloo, SE1 8SQ. Telephone 020 7928 6196 **New**
Gaffer: Chris Elliott
Food: Good traditional food cooked to order 12 to 7.30, 12 to 4 Sun
Smoking Throughout
Open: 11 to 11, 12 to 10.30 Sun

The Hole in the Wall is a pub underneath the Arches immediately outside the main entrance to Waterloo Station. It has, therefore, some very unusual design features and a character that is like few others in Britain. There are two rooms, one small and snug the other large and canteen like, both with the rumble of overhead railways to agitate the beer.

MP – SKY – JB

This Freehouse has been in the same family for a very long time. In its present form it is well known for offering rarer ales, on my visit it was the Battersea ale that drew my eye. Whenever I have gone in it has been very busy. The people are fairly transient so it is best to go into the back room where there is space and often a table to sit around and watch sports on the large TV. Ian the Morton fan of a manager was keen to stress that this is a no colours pub and that the locals are very much regular commuters. Many will be Railway workers of the Eurostar type. Andy my train driving mate being one such advocate of the HITW. On Rugby international days the pub will be heaving, so too when away fans are travelling home and wanting a quick pint before the train home. The bar menu will be limited on such days but the beer menu likely to be at its most extensive. It has a heart in the traditions of a proper London Boozer. a good welcome and conversation is guaranteed at any time of the day.

BWV 22.3.06: Adnams *Best, Broadside*, Battersea *Bitter*, Fuller's *London Pride*, Shepherd Neame *Spitfire*, Young's *Bitter, Special*

Mad Bishop and Bear

The Lawn, Paddington Station, W2 1HB. Telephone 020 740 22441
Gaffer: David and Chad
Food: Traditional pub-food from pastries to steaks 9 to 9
Separate smoking areas
Open: 9 to 11 Mon to Fri, 7.30 to 11 Sat, 10 to 10.30 Sun

In my opinion this is the best designed London station bar. It takes elements of classic pub design (tiled floors and mirrors, etc.) and integrates them into a large, modern terminus waiting bar, complete with two plasma screens for TV matches. The good, friendly staff and quality ale make this ideal for meeting up

MP – TV – BM – D

and planning your visit to London. Large and comfortable, but retaining the design features that allow for quiet supping, the Mad Bishop and Bear is whatever you want it to be. As a footie fan you might need to dodge the crowds of fellow fans in colours to be allowed through Sushi land to the bar. Alternatively, for London fans going west catch a breakfast and beer before the train journey out west. Sit on the terrace to get the full interest of being in one of GWR's beautiful stations.
UPDATE: Clare has moved on – most be something in the beer! The pub is as busy as ever. I visited half a dozen times over the season and it never disappointed.

BWV 20.12.04: Fuller's *Chiswick, ESB, London Porter, London Pride*
BWV 1.2.06: Fuller's *Chiswick, Discovery, ESB, London Pride*

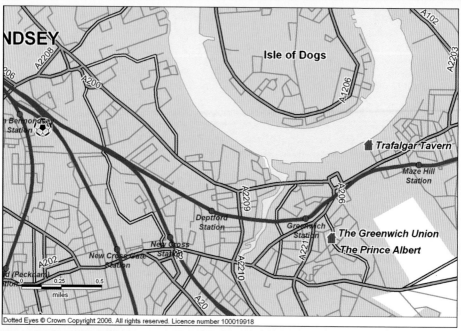

Isle of Dogs

Trafalgar Tavern

Maze Hill Station

Deptford Station

Greenwich Station

The Greenwich Union

The Prince Albert

New Cross Station

New Cross Gate Station

MP | TV | BM | D

Ashburnham Arms

25 Ashburnham Grove Greenwich, SE10 8UH. Telephone 020 8692 2057
Gaffers: Denis Ryan and Nalaka Kapuru
**Food: All home cooked international menu 12 to 2.30, 6 to 9 Tue to Sat,
12 to 8 Sun, No food Mon**
Separate smoking areas
Open: 12 to 11

New

B

The Ashburnham is the most modern of the real ale locals in the Greenwich station area. By modern I mean that it is refurbished with all the features of recent pub design, yet it has managed to maintain the essential qualities of being a real pub with log fires and great ale.

Denis and Nalaka have created a friendly and welcoming community pub where families are very much at the heart of what they do. It helps to have one of the few play – streets outside the pub and a garden area that is both enclosed and has very recently been decked and heated. The locals really appreciate these attributes but it would be true to say that the Ashburnham is a great example of how to cater for all ages and sexes through good ale and food. To encourage the community feel the pub is frequently the host to interest and sporting groups. The local bell ringers, beer festival organisers, quiz teams and a pub cricket side; all are important in making the pub a place to meet other people or people watch. The regulars tend to be professional couples and local artisans. The football fans will support teams across London. On Saturday the mix will be very friendly, as was found last year by supporters of Leyton Orient and Manchester City. Charlton fans call in before, using the DLR or main line trains, just five minutes away.

BWV 28.3.06: Shepherd Neame *Early Bird, Kent's Best, Master Brew, Spitfire*

The Prince Albert

72 Royal Hill, Greenwich SE10 8RT. Telephone 020 8333 6512 **New**
Gaffers: Peter and Janet Clements
Food: All home cooked traditional pub food 12 to 3 Mon to Fri
Pies and pasties at weekend
Smoking Throughout
Open: 11 to 11.30 Mon to Sat, 11.30 to 11.30 Sun

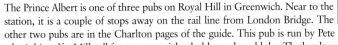

The Prince Albert is one of three pubs on Royal Hill in Greenwich. Near to the station, it is a couple of stops away on the rail line from London Bridge. The other two pubs are in the Charlton pages of the guide. This pub is run by Pete who is himself a Millwall fan, a season ticket holder and top bloke. The locals are very friendly and the atmosphere both sporty and traditional.

The pub is a bit of a rarity in that it has two self-contained rooms both upstairs and down that are used for pool. The main bar has Sky TV that is strictly for the use of sports fans, there is no watching countdown in this pub. The support for community sports continues through sponsorship of local teams and regular connections to Blackheath Rugby Club, their players and supporters. The pub is also a place where local students come for their first pints only to find it is a proper local, no themes, no gimmicks; a local that if you treat it right will be your local for life. On my mid afternoon visit the Prince was buzzing. There were some watching the racing but most regulars were doing Greenwich things. There were people sketching scenes from the bar, others comparing thoughts on the national curriculum and most just supping over a good book. The pub gets very busy on matchdays but has the space to accommodate this. I really liked the busy nature of the pub and especially the keenness of the staff to make this stranger welcome.

BWV 28.3.06: Adnams *Broadside*, Courage *Best*, Greene King *IPA*

Trafalgar Tavern

6 Park Row Road, Greenwich, SE10 9NW. Telephone 020 8858 2909 **New**
www.trafalgartavern.co.uk
Gaffer: Mick Abrahams
Food: Traditional English/European menu, all home cooked
12 to 3, 6 to 10 in restaurant, 12 to 10.30 in bar
Smoking Throughout
Open: 12 to 11 Mon to Thu, 12 to 1am Fri and Sat, 12 to 10.30 Sun

The Trafalgar Tavern must be one of the most impressively located pubs in urban Britain. It is a grand mansion of a pub, literally on the river bank with the façade of Greenwich University as the next door neighbour. Across the river lies the Isle of Dogs and then downstream the Millennium Dome It is no surprise then to hear that 80% of the trade is tourist related and similarly large proportions of the trade here is in food and ale taken by people who come for the fantastic views from the picture windows in the pub.

It is more than just a glorified restaurant though. It is equally distinctive inside. The building is made up of 5 large, high ceilinged drawing rooms from a classical country house. Four of those rooms are designed for maximum access to the views out of the windows. In the evening the numerous walkers give way to the locals who will be local professional couples enjoying a meal and a few beers On my lunchtime visit people came and went moving from table to table at times, just to get pole position. Conversation was very much Canary Wharf orientated; either that or based on the state of British education. It has a definite air of sophistication without become pretentious. I would enjoy this pub if doing the tourist things in Greenwich over the weekend. It is not a typical footie fans pub, but as an alternative for a great location and a good meal, this is just, well as I said, impressive.

BWV 28.3.06: Adnams *Best*, Flowers *IPA*, Fuller's *London Porter*, *London Pride*

CULTURAL GUIDES

Millwall

For nearly two thousand years London was linked to the south by just one bridge. The Thames' south bank was literally beyond the pale. A Roman gladiator's trident found here suggests South Londoners have enjoyed watching blokes trying to kill each other for a long time, and the fact that there were once seven prisons confirms a reputation for lawlessness. There were also theatres, inns and lots of prostitutes, many of them paying rent to the Bishop of Winchester and other prelates. Our cathedrals may have been built to the glory of God but many were helped by the muck of man.

When Millwall FC moved south of the Thames, from the Isle of Dogs, in 1910 most of the fun had been driven out of the area by industrialisation. The away end at the old Den could only be reached along narrow, railway shrouded alleys. The New Den, and the area around, still feels more like 'industry, corrugated and grim' than any other ground we know; but there seems less chance of getting lost, stabbed and dumped in a scrap yard car crusher walking to it. Having said that the South Bank is booming again, and most of London's newly built tourist attractions are here. We suspect that rich people are going to discover that there's money to be made from the grim, cheap land around Millwall FC. Which may then find itself in a fashionable area: however we doubt the club will ever abandon the area's traditions.

Northampton

If you ignore the north, as many Southerners do, then Northampton is bang in the middle of England. This made it politically and economically important in the Middle Ages. Several Parliaments were held here, and it then became famous for cobblers. The market is impressive and the museum has a world class shoe collection.

During the Napoleonic Wars Northampton's centrality, or rather its distance from the sea, resulted in the British Government picking the barracks at Weeton Bec, just to the west, to be where they and the King would bolt to if Boney's army had landed. With victory at Trafalgar in 1805 there was little chance of that, but it was kept ready as a refuge, and served as a gunpowder and uniform storehouse. A cut was made to the nearby Grand Union Canal, complete with portcullised gatehouses. The military left in 1961 but much remains. The writer Byron Rogers claims this would be the ideal starting place for an armed rising, but you need to be quick, before it is turned into posh housing for TV producers, bureaucrats and politicians fleeing from the boney poor of our cities.

'Perhaps the most imposing architectural monument of the 7th century yet surviving north of the Alps'
Sir Alfred Clapham.

Brixworth Church

You will not be visiting Brixworth village, north of Northampton, if shopping malls are the only buildings that excite you, or 1966 is the earliest historical date you remember. For the rest: this is a stunning building.

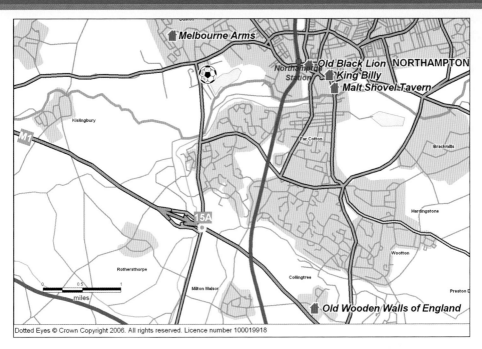

Dotted Eyes © Crown Copyright 2006. All rights reserved. Licence number 100019918

King Billy

2 Commercial Street, NN1 1PJ. Telephone 01604 621325 **New**
Gaffer: Rachel Morgan
Food: Good value traditional menu with themed burger menu a feature
12 to 2.30, 6 to 9 Mon to Fri, 12 to 6 Sat and Sun
Smoking Throughout
Open: 12 to 11 Sun to Wed, 12 to 12 Thu to Sat

| MP | JB | PG | D |

Ray was given the brief of finding two Northampton town centre pubs with a difference and the King Billy certainly fits the bill. It is a large single-bar pub that stands out from the crowd for its friendly rocky atmosphere. It is the epitome of the modern biker pub, i.e. full of caring people who know what makes a good time for them, and welcoming to those who wish to join in the fun.

The bar is arranged on different levels and, as the photo showsm was under the process of being renovated when we visited. Like all the best pubs of this type real ale plays a big part alongside Jack Daniels, Newcastle Brown ale and live music. The pub is peculiarly decorated with dark walls that are a must when the music is played at the weekends. There are also regular music festivals hosted at the pub, the following Sunday for example has ten bands playing throughout the day. It is also a traditional pub in the very best style. It may be odd to see push bikes in the bar and motor bikes in the pub garden; yet the locals also include the good old and young boys who like a good pint. The beers are ever-changing from the very best of national selections. Rachel is very enthusiastic about this pub and her style is everywhere. It is a fun pub of the best type, one that favourably contrasts with the others found in Northampton.

BWV 26.5.06: Black Sheep *Bitter,* Fuller's *Gale's Festival,* **London Pride,** Greene King *IPA, Old Speckled Hen,* Wadworth *6X,* Young's *Waggledance*

SP

Malt Shovel Tavern

121 Bridge Street, NN1 1QF. Telephone 01604 234212
www.themaltshoveltavern.com
Gaffer: Norman Tetzlaff-Murrell
Food: Light bites menu and a range of special meals 12 to 2.30 Mon to Sat
Smoking Throughout
Open: 11.30 to 3, 5 to 11 Mon to Sat, 12 to 3, 7 to 12.30 Sun

The Malt Shovel is well recommended by rugby rather than footie fans. *'If the Saints are at home it gets very crowded.'* One would be led to think that they have this as a second home away from Frankland Gardens. It is a large wood and brick one bar tavern with a widely known reputation for quality ales. The owners' love of real ale comes through in the beer memorabilia. This is a rightly popular haunt for ale travellers, myself included, who have often caught the train to Northampton with this pub as the Holy Grail. You even get a *'scratch and sniff'* experience from the brewery opposite. It was East Midlands pub of the year 2004, has regular blues nights and, something I recall with affection; it offers Gale's Country wines for a different experience.
UPDATE: Look out for the pubs' own Great Oakley brews.

BWV 16.11.04 Banks's **Bitter**, Blindmans **Siberia**, Frog Island **Natterjack**, **Golden Hill**, Exmoor **Wildcat**, RCH **Old Slug Porter**, Tetley's **Cask Bitter**, Westcroft **Cider**
BWV 19.11.05: Frog Island **Natterjack**, Fuller's **London Pride**, Great Oakley **Harpers**, **Tail Shaker**, Nethergate **Old Growler**, Oakham **Bishops Farewell**, **JHB**, Stonehouse **Old Smokey**, Tetley's **Cask Bitter**, Vale **Black Swan Mild**, **Special**

CP TV JB PG

Melbourne Arms

Melbourne Lane, Duston, NN5 6HS. Telephone 01604 752837
Gaffer: Ken Morris
Smoking Throughout
Open: 11 to 11 Mon to Thu, 11 to 12 Fri and Sat, 12 to 10.30 Sun

There are three regular beers on offer in this village pub. It has the feel of a local's pub with pool table and sports team trophies. The low beams and stone walls help to give a warm feeling as does the chat with local fans. *'Parking is an issue everywhere in Northampton so it might be a good idea to finish up here and walk down to the ground'* My visit found the regulars settling in for the afternoon TV racing session. A good hour later the numbers hadn't changed, neither had the number of winners, none. They told me the usual thing on a Saturday was to walk through the local estate to the ground, thus avoiding the congestion of warehouse shoppers mixing in with the lack of traffic control at the ground. This is a typical Northamptonshire pub in a village that has managed to keep some of its identity as the town has grown around it. Ken was very tolerant of my intrusion to the normal lunchtime activities, cheers Ken.
UPDATE: The Melbourne is totally unchanged.

BWV 16.11.04: Courage **Directors**, **Best**, Fuller's **London Pride**
BWV 26.5.06: Caledonian **Deuchars IPA**, Courage **Best**, **Directors**, Wells **Bombardier**

Old Black Lion

1 Black Lion Hill, NN1 1SW. Telephone 01604 639472
Gaffer: Steven Wilkinson
Smoking Throughout
Open: 12 to 11 Mon to Sat, 12 to 10.30 Sun

The Old Black Lion is located on the main route from the railway station to the town centre. It looks like a traditional old fashioned pub from the outside, especially when seen with the parish church next door. It is therefore, a bit of a surprise when one enters, to find that the pub has a modern design; bright painted walls and an open plan layout that includes steps down into a separate lounge.

I really liked this recommendation. Steven has returned to the pub and has plans to build up the trade based on good real ale and in the future quality food. The ale includes my favourite Frog Island ales, from the brewery along the road. No doubt there will be an increase the number of office workers and lunchtime trade. At present the pub is very much a locals and regulars pub, a bit of a guarded secret. The sports fans are catered for by large screens and a pull down version. Those fans are more likely to appreciate rugby than the Cobblers, as appears common among the real ale drinkers in this town. It can get busy before the game if fans arrive by train. As with all the town pubs it is a long hike to the ground, but here the taxis at the station will be easier to find. Ray had succeeded in his quest and we settled to a beer while watching the window cleaner rather than me thrashing him at pool as usual.

BWV 26.5.06: Courage *Best*, Frog Island *Natterjack, Shoemaker*

Old Wooden Walls of England

25 High Street, Collingtree, NN4 0NE. Telephone 01604 764082
Gaffer: Melvin Howles
Food: Traditional Pub food with a rustic touch
12 to 3, 6 to 9 Mon to Sat, 12 to 4 Sun
Separate smoking areas
Open: 12 to 3, 5 to 11 Mon to Sat, 12 to 10.30 Sun

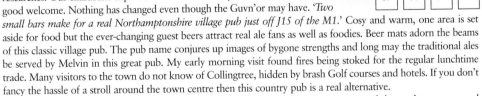

This pub is also a long standing destination of our Milton Keynes based real ale researches. Our charabanc trips would arrive here early doors as it always had a good welcome. Nothing has changed even though the Guvn'or may have. *'Two small bars make for a real Northamptonshire village pub just off J15 of the M1.'* Cosy and warm, one area is set aside for food but the ever-changing guest beers attract real ale fans as well as foodies. Beer mats adorn the beams of this classic village pub. The pub name conjures up images of bygone strengths and long may the traditional ales be served by Melvin in this great pub. My early morning visit found fires being stoked for the regular lunchtime trade. Many visitors to the town do not know of Collingtree, hidden by brash Golf courses and hotels. If you don't fancy the hassle of a stroll around the town centre then this country pub is a real alternative.
UPDATE: Melvin arrived in July and things are changing. The pub has a new menu and the gardens are opened up for families to enjoy.

BWV 16.11.04: Banks's *Bitter*, Camerons *Strongarm*, Hook Norton *Old Hooky*, Marston's *Pedigree*
BWV 19.11.05: Banks's *Bitter*, Hook Norton *Old Hooky*, Jennings *Cocker Hoop*, Marston's *Pedigree*

LEAGUE TABLES

The league tables are given because many of you may only travel to a few games away from home a season. When you do it might involve an overnight stay or a full weekend of beer drinking research and a game. The table should give you the readers choices of which are the best towns and those that might best be left for another year.

The scoring is based on a very crude analysis of:

1   The average number of beers on offer when I visited each pub ABP (Average beer points).

2   A weighted score based on the number of votes each town received when I asked the people to rate their top three towns for football and real ale WVS (Weighted vote score).

3   I then fixed it to get my personal choices at the top.

4   The end result is something that should not be taken too seriously

PREMIERSHIP

	ABP	WVS	TOTAL
NEWCASTLE	4.5	15	19.5
MAN CITY	8	5	13
PORTSMOUTH	5.3	5	10.3
SHEFFIELD U	7	3	10
TOTTENHAM	7.6	2	9.6
MAN UNITED	3.5	5	8.5
ASTON VILLA	7.4	0	7.4
EVERTON	7	0	7
BOLTON	4.2	2	6.2
CHELSEA	4	2	6
WEST HAM	4	2	6
LIVERPOOL	5.6	0	5.6
BLACKBURN	3.4	2	5.4
ARSENAL	3	2	5
READING	4.75	0	4.75
FULHAM	2.66	2	4.66
WATFORD	4.6	0	4.6
CHARLTON	2.33	2	4.33
MIDDLESBORO	2.8	1	3.8
WIGAN	3.6	0	3.6

CHAMPIONSHIP

	ABP	WVS	TOTAL
DERBY	7.1	9	16.1
NORWICH	11.4	2	13.4
SHEFFIELD W	9	4	13
IPSWICH	10.7	1	11.7
BIRMINGHAM	8.7	0	8.7
WEST BROM	3.6	5	8.6
LEEDS	8	0	8
SOUTHAMPTON	6	1	7
BURNLEY	5.5	1	6.5
LEICESTER	6.2	0	6.2
SUNDERLAND	5.7	0	5.7
COVENTRY	5.6	0	5.6
WOLVES	5.5	0	5.5
STOKE	5.4	0	5.4
PRESTON	5	0	5
CARDIFF	5	0	5
HULL	4.9	0	4.9
LUTON	4.8	0	4.8
SOUTHEND	4.5	0	4.5
PLYMOUTH	4.5	0	4.5
BARNSLEY	4.2	0	4.2
COLCHESTER	4	0	4
QPR	3.33	0	3.33
CRYSTAL PALACE	2.66	0	2.66

DIVISION ONE

	ABP	WVS	TOTAL
NOTTINGHAM F	9.1	6	15.1
BRADFORD	8.7	2	10.7
HUDDERSFIELD	7.8	2	9.8
CHESTERFIELD	8.1	0	8.1
BLACKPOOL	5	3	8
LEYTON ORIENT	5	2	7
BRISTOL C	5.2	1	6.2
BRIGHTON	6	0	6
MILLWALL	3.66	2	5.66
NORTHAMPTON	5.1	0	5.1
TRANMERE	5.1	0	5.1
ROTHERHAM	5	0	5
DONCASTER	4.8	0	4.8
PORT VALE	4.7	0	4.7
SWANSEA	4.6	0	4.6
BOURNEMOUTH	4.6	0	4.6
CREWE	4.6	0	4.6
CHELTENHAM	4.4	0	4.4
GILLINGHAM	4.1	0	4.1
SCUNTHORPE	4	0	4
BRENTFORD	4	0	4
OLDHAM	3.4	0	3.4
YEOVIL	3	0	3
CARLISLE	2.6	0	2.6

DIVISION TWO

	ABP	WVS	TOTAL
PETERBOROUGH	9.4	8	17.4
LINCOLN	6	8	14
NOTTS CO	7.5	6	13.5
SHREWSBURY	6.4	7	13.4
DARLINGTON	6.8	4	10.8
STOCKPORT	8.6	1	9.6
CHESTER	4.6	4	8.6
WALSALL	6.8	0	6.8
HEREFORD	6.6	0	6.6
BRISTOL R	5.5	1	6.5
MANSFIELD	6	0	6
BURY	5.6	0	5.6
ROCHDALE	4.3	1	5.3
SWINDON	5.25	0	5.25
GRIMSBY	5	0	5
MACCLESFIELD	3.8	1	4.8
BOSTON	4	0	4
TORQUAY	3.8	0	3.8
MILTON KEYNES	3.75	0	3.75
WYCOMBE	3.5	0	3.5
ACCRINGTON	3.3	0	3.3
BARNET	3	0	3
HARTLEPOOL	2.5	0	2.5
WREXHAM	2	0	2

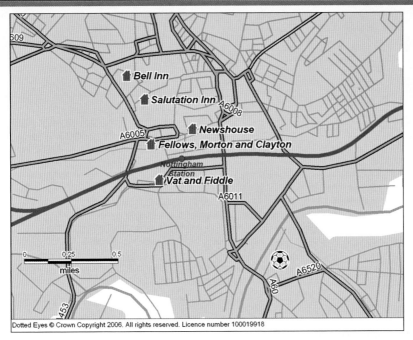

Dotted Eyes © Crown Copyright 2006. All rights reserved. Licence number 100019918

Bell Inn

18 Angel Row, NG1 6HL Telephone 0115 9475241
www.thebell-inn.com
Gaffer: Brian Rigby
Food: Full menu of snacks and main meals 12 to 8 bar, 6 to 9.30 restaurant
No smoking restaurant
Open: 10.30 to late. 12 to late Sun

MP | BM

I'm not normally keen to try pubs in the main town square, but the Bell is a must-do experience. The impressive frontage is magnetic; inside the place has a Tardis-like effect. A passage-way separates two small bars that in themselves would make a great town location. Then a back door leads into a much larger hall of a room, all wood-panelled and reminding me of a redbrick Junior Common Room. In this room were the serious real ale fans, sampling the tail end of their beer festival. Evidence of regular blues music catches the eye for evening entertainment, but the most impressive factor was the general air of reflective reverence for a great town-pub environment and a rarer range of real ales.

UPDATE: A small outside area has been added. It has live music Mon and Thu evenings, cave and building tours on Tuesdays. A real ale festival is due at Christmas. It was CAMRA pub of excellence 2005.

BWV 23.3.05: Burton Bridge *Damson Porter*, Hardys and Hanson *Kimberley Mild*, *Kimberley Bitter*, *Olde Trip*, *Peddlers Pride*, *William Clarke Strong Ale*, Hilden Brewing Co. *Silver*, Maguire's *Rusty Irish Red*, *Haus*
BWV 20.10.05: Hardys and Hanson *Kimberley Bitter*, *Kimberley Mild*, *Olde Trip*, *William Clarke Strong Ale*

SP SKY BM PG D

Newshouse

123 Canal Street, NG1 7HB. Telephone 0115 9502419
Gaffer: Bob Fairclough
Food: Fresh Rolls From 11
Smoking Throughout
Open: 11 to 11

The Newshouse is a top pub of the old kind. It has real locals of all professions, ages and interests. It offers a lounge and a bar complete with darts board and bar skittles. Most importantly, the ales come from beyond the predictable norm and are in great condition. My visit found teachers, printers and posties among others chatting around the bar over a post-work beer. The walls have Forest cuttings and other items from the alleged days of the place being a reading room for the local illiterate. I particularly enjoyed the bar tiles proclaiming the names of regional independent brewers. All in all this is a great town pub, in an area with few residents, which suggests the nearby station and tram provides the link to home and town party venues. I just had to go back later to play the bar billiards near to last orders and get some Black Bear to round off a perfect day.
UPDATE: Plans are afoot for an extension to the rear in the next few years.

BWV 23.3.05: Beartown *Black Bear*, Coach House *Rabbit Punch*, Crouch Vale *Blackwater Mild*, Everards *Perfick*, *Harvest Pale*, Hop Back *Summer Lightning*, Weston's *Old Rosie*
BWV 20.10.05: Castle Rock *Daily Gold*, *Hemlock*, Everards *Tiger*, Rebellion *Mutiny*, Mauldons *Suffolk Pride*, Moles *Rucking Mole*, Weston's *Old Rosie Cider*

MP SKY BM D

Fellows, Morton and Clayton

54 Canal Street, NG1 7EX Telephone 0115 9506795
www.fellowsmortonandclayton.co.uk
Gaffer: Graham Jackson
Food: Extensive bar and restaurant menu 11.30 to 9, 12 to 6 Sun
No smoking at the bar and non smoking section
Open: 11 to 11, 11 to 12 Fri and Sat

The FMC is my most-recommended Nottingham pub and it is easy to see why. A canal-side and town-street location, near to the station, gives it both tourist and townie appeal. It brews its own ales, the examples here having interesting variations. The pub itself extends to the canal by means of a conservatory bar and outside tables/patio at various different levels. My visit found a large number of office workers and shoppers mingling with real ale buffs chasing new brews. What struck me was the age of those ale drinkers; the FMC is breeding a younger generation of real ale drinkers. It is a top pub, one to remember and tell your mates about. This is also the prefect weekend away pub, great on Friday evenings.
UPDATE: New landlord Graham hosted the launch of the Nottingham beer festival

BWV 23.3.05: Caledonian *Deuchars IPA*, Camerons *Castle Eden Ale*, Fellows, Morton and Clayton *Fellows*, *Post Haste*, Fuller's *London Pride*, Mallards *Duckling*, Timothy Taylor *Landlord*
BWV 20.10.05: Caledonian *Deuchars IPA*, Camerons *Castle Eden Ale*, Clark's *Classic Blonde*, Fellow, Morton and Clayton *Fellows*, *Post Haste*, Fuller's *London Pride*, Nottingham *Legend*

Salutation Inn

Maid Marian Way, NG1 7AA. Telephone 0115 9589432
Gaffer: Gary Minford
Food: Delicious home cooked traditional food 11 to 7 Mon to Sat, 12 to 6 Sun
Separate smoking areas
Open: 11 to 11 Mon to Sat, 12 to 10.30 Sun

Tourists, and those outside the town, recommend the nearby Trip to Jerusalem. Locals and, indeed, myself prefer the nearby Salutation. The visit showed me why the locals prefer it. At lunch-time groups of women from nearby offices and blokes on shopping trips were sampling real ales and enjoying good food in a pub that has plenty of historic values and is a real pub to boot. The bar on Maid Marian Way is larger and roomier, yet has hiding places for couples and solitary drinkers, like myself that day. The entrance from the back-street finds a passage and cosy rooms, timber-framed and full of the character one comes to expect in Nottingham. While the pub has TV and music, it is all very discrete. Footie is unlikely to be shown, whereas rugby, especially Irish games, is more likely to get a crowd in.

UPDATE: A new chef has arrived from the Falcon. It also has live bands, quizzes, karaoke and pub machine games.

BWV 23.3.05: Bass *Draught*, Brakspear *Special*, Caledonian *80/-*, Everards *Tiger*, Shepherd Neame *Masterbrew*, Tetley's *Cask Bitter*, Wells *Bombardier*
BWV 20.10.05: Adnams *Broadside*, Badger *Tanglefoot*, Camerons *Castle Eden Ale*, Marston's *Pedigree*, Weston's *Old Rosie Cider*

Vat and Fiddle

12 Queens Bridge Road, NG2 1NB. Telephone 0115 9580611
Gaffer: Sarah Houghton
Food: Light snack Panini's and chillie 12 to 2.30
Smoking Throughout
Open: 11 to 11, 11 to 12 at weekends

The Vat and Fiddle looks out of place in its town street location. The building is in a style of suburban roadside pubs, complete with being set back from the road. The interior is simply superb, simply laid out, simply a great place to sample great real ale. The pub is the tap room outlet for Castle Rock ales and the range here certainly included rarities that I had yet to sample. Belgian bottled beers and guests add to the range, so no wonder my visit found real ale hunters from far and wide essentially making a pilgrimage.

UPDATE: There are plans to extend the pub and, with it, the range of food that is available. Sarah arrived from the Swan and Rushes in Loughborough. It was a great place to visit this year before the Nottingham beer festival. Those coming off the train headed here first, chatted about the ale scene and the general decline in local football fortunes, before heading off for a great session.

BWV 23.3.05: Archers *Golden*, Beartown *Bearcross*, Castle Rock *Meadows Gold*, Hemlock *Bitter*, *Harvest Pale*, *Elsie Mo*, *Painted Lady*, Crouch Vale *Blackwater Mild*, Dark Star *Original*
BWV 20.10.05: Brewster's *Marquis*, Castle Rock *Elsie Mo*, *Harvest Pale*, *Hemlock Bitter*, *Hemlock Gold*, Crouch Vale *Blackwater Mild*, *Deck Aid*, Mauldon's *Black Adder*, Moles *Molegrip*, Newby Wyke *Black Squall*, Saxon *Ruby Tuesday Cider*

Nottingham Forest

In Portrait of the River Trent Peter Lord describes Nottingham as:

'Perched on the twin breasts of its unique site, one nippled by its castle and the other by its great parish church, the old Nottingham was content to leave the broad, low marshlands on its southern flank to the vagaries of the river and to the blue crocus.'

Castle Hill became the French borough. Church Hill became the English borough. The two made the City of Nottingham, north of the River Trent, site of Notts County's Meadow Lane. Nottingham Forest's Trent Bridge on the south bank was in the county of Nottinghamshire!?

The Castle

Little medieval remains, but much happened here, including the Civil War's official start: but the best story involves Isabella, Queen of England and her lover Roger Mortimer.

In his Dictionary of English Queens, JL Carr writes: *'Isabella of France; (d. 1358, aged 65), Shakespeare's 'she wolf', a very amorous woman wasted on Edward II who gave her wedding presents to him to men friends.'*

Helped by Lord Mortimer, she imprisoned her husband and arranged his murder by inserting a red hot wire into his bowels through a horn tube (so as to leave no mark). Mortimer then ruled in the son's name, but in October 1330, 14 year old Edward III and a few soldiers entered the Castle through one of many rock passages, and dragged Mortimer and the Queen from bed. Mortimer was executed and Isabella set to a nunnery.

Oldham

Oldham people always seem friendly and ever ready to talk to strangers, although even a stranger bred in Manchester may struggle to understand them. We wish we could be positive about the town for their sake, but after an exchange of e-mails with Oldham Council, which ended with receipt of a lecture on how to work their unworkable clockwork website, we cannot do so this year.

Oldham was once a rich cotton town and Oldham Athletic were a founder member of the Premiership. Both have clearly suffered from lost glory, and poor leadership and judgement. We wonder if Oldham Athletic regrets helping the breakaway Premiership change football so the lower leagues were left to rot.

Oldham is almost surrounded by hills but only a short way from Manchester. The moors offer fine walks but prevented expansion. It tried to keep up with its bigger neighbours but beggared itself in trying. It has an expensive road system that cuts the centre off, but is still difficult to drive through. It has fine buildings, but more were knocked down, leaving a confused patchwork. The train service is also confusing and the 'main' station sits forlornly in a retail park.

Museum and Art Gallery

These were excellent, but were closed down; and the start of our Oldham argument was because their website gave no facts about its future. We have heard rumours that the new facility is open and impressive, but you will have to check details for yourself.

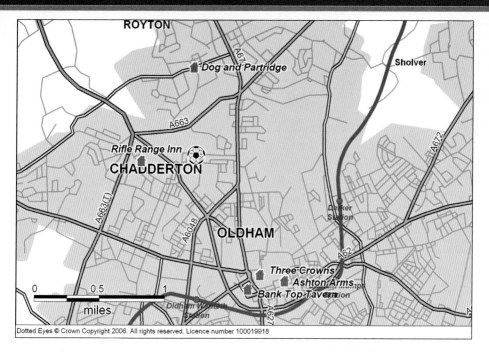

Dotted Eyes © Crown Copyright 2006. All rights reserved. Licence number 100019918

Ashton Arms

28-30 Clegg Street, OL1 1PL. Telephone 0161 6309789
Gaffer: Jo Potter
Food Wholesome home cooked bar food 12 to 6 Mon to Thu, 12 to 3 Fri
Smoking Throughout
Open: 11.30 to 11 Mon to Thu, 11.30 to 11.30 Fri/Sat, 11.30 to 10.30 Sun

The pub opened in its present form in October 2003 having been one of the few
Porters outlets. It is the home of the Oldham real ale fan clubs having regular
changes of ales that keep the drinker who wants variety amply satisfied.
Arranged like an extended comfortable lounge it has sofas for relaxed chat and
more traditional stools and tables for those who feast on ales and sandwiches. While alcohol may well be the cause
and cure of my problems (*Homer Simpson*) this pub is patently the great hall of ale in the Oldham real ale scene.
It is a great town centre boozer with a very homely touch. The pub always has a range of ales like that listed below
and is also renowned at being an outlet for Millstone ales, one of my favourite northern microbrews, unfortunately
not on my visit though. It didn't matter as the alternative was fine as was the locals company was fun.
UPDATE: The list of ales now stands over 1000, shed loads by any standards. The pub is also recognised in the
Good Cider Guide. Guess what, buses stop outside.

BWV 11.2.05: Brewster's *Rutterkin*, Greenfield *Dobcross*, Pictish *Porter*, Mauldons *Moletrap*, Boggart Hole
Clough *Bunny Boiler*, Hydes *Satisfaction*, Weston's *Cider*
BWV 27.4.06: Brewster's *Belly Dancer*, Copper Dragon *Black Gold*, Marston Moor *Purveyor General*, Rudgate
Starling, Shaws *IPA*, Woodland *Midnight Stout*

MP | TV | JB | D

Bank Top Tavern

King Square, OL8 1ES. Telephone 0161 6248603

Gaffers: Terry and Pearl Morrison

Food: Home made and cheap good quality pub food 10 to 2 Mon to Sat, 10 to 5 Sun

Separate smoking areas

Open: 10 to 12

Terry and Pearl have run the Bank Top for many years often being recognised by the local CAMRA members as a great local with a very friendly traditional feel. It is located near the Mecca Bingo Hall, an area of town that is likely to change dramatically over the next few years as the local college develops University status. The pub is large and rambles around to the back where a large area has been set aside for a proper pub restaurant. As with many other pubs in the town there is a redecoration/refurbishment started. This will not change what is essentially a very friendly family orientated pub. In JW Lees country the pubs have very little option with guest ales. The selection of the Bank Top comes from the unlucky residents of Oldham who recommend it for the quality of the ale and its real atmosphere. It is supplemented by seasonal ales when they are available. A function room is another that would be great for meetings of community groups as well as the usual wedding party/disco activities. Terry doubles as karaoke king and DJ at the weekend. At this time the students will have finished nursing a pint between two and the locals will have started the fun associated with a typical fun pub of the older variety. Don't expect any modern bar frills, it is an honest boozer that will never disappoint. The locals will be friendly and Latic, but talk rugby league and you are more likely to find genuine enthusiasm.

BWV 27.4.06: Lees *Bitter, GB Mild*

CP | TV | BM | PG | D

Dog and Partridge

148 Middleton Road, Royton, OL2 5LL. Telephone 0161 6206403

Gaffers: Neil Jackson and Rita Thompson

Smoking Throughout

Open: 4 to 12 Mon to Thu, 12 to 1am Fri and Sat, 12 to 10.30 Sun

The Dog and Partridge is a pub that I had not visited for many years because the Latics and my team have parted company. It was with real relish that I made the trek from town to see how it had changed. The answer I found was that it was friendly, cosy, and traditional; just as I remembered it. The Lees ale included my favourite mild and the legacy of having a long established Guvn'or was obvious it this much loved and sparkling local.

Rita is herself a football fan. A club shirt holds centre stage above the fire in the larger carpeted main lounge. The pub has three rooms, the front two both having a dart board and bench seating around the walls. Most will congregate in the lounge, spotlessly clean and in the much-loved brass and dinner plate style. The pub has been recommended by many fans that enjoy the fact that it takes a detour from the main routes to find. The locals are very welcoming. The best plan is to ask their advice re the best way to walk through the estates to the ground. It is apparently less than 15 minutes, behind the now non productive Mill that lies to the rear. Of course the regulars include lost United and City fans and a fair number of the oval game devotees. Quizzes, karaoke and live music vary the community activities. My visit was the first hot day of the year and the cool of the bar was very welcome. If you only have time for one Lees pub then this will be the best if you like to meet similar minded real ale fans who also like to find something just a bit different, yet recognisable.

BWV 27.4.06: Lees *Bitter, GB Mild*

Rifle Range Inn

372 Burnley Lane, OL1 2QP. Telephone 0161 6265543
Gaffers: Ann and Jim Humphries
Smoking Throughout
Open: 12 to 11, 12 to 10.30 Sun

CP | SKY | JB | PG | D

As one of the most recommended footie and ale pubs this is a place that away fans return to every year. It is convenient, a short walk to the ground and for a quick post-match getaway to the motorway. The pub is very customer orientated. It has two TV screens for the lunchtime matches, plenty of comfortable space and, best of all; Anne has been known to provide free food for the faithful who need something warm at what is reputedly the coldest ground in the country. On non-matchdays the memorial board is of interest to locals as is the picture of Prince Charles sampling Lees' ales. I liked the overall feel of the place, more country farmhouse than town boozer, more family than blokes only. So if you have time to visit just one pub then the Rifle Range will provide a great welcome, a chance to mix with friendly locals and maybe best of all, no hassle involved in walking around the rather beer desolate town centre. There is a field at the back of the pub which acts as a car park so it is worth getting there early as an away fan.
UPDATE: Beer is the same good quality; the pub is in the process of redecoration.

BWV 11.2.05: Lees *Mild, Bitter*.
BWV 27.4.06: Lees *Bitter, GB Mild*

Three Crowns **New**

1-3 Manchester Chambers, Manchester Street, OL1 1LE.
Telephone 0161 6289301
Gaffer: Paul Ratcliffe
Food: High quality, locally sourced home cooked menu
11 to 5.30 Mon to Fri, 11 to 3 Sat and Sun
Separate smoking areas
Open: 11 to 11, 12 to 11 Sun

F

MP | TV | BM | PG | D

When you visit the Three Crowns expect the beer list to have increased and the place to be even busier than reported to me. My visit found Paul in the difficult process of establishing his identity on the pub. He moved in a week before and already the locals had noticed the improvement and the good word was spreading.

The Crowns is very impressive, both internally and externally. The timber framed shell has a surprisingly light interior. You can play '*Jackanory*' with the windows. Through the rectangular window you get a view of the new bus stations. (How many does a town need?) The square windows reveal the red wall of the shopping precinct. Then, glory of glories, through the magnificent arched windows, is the Crown Court. The pub is essentially one big room but certainly not simple in design. Ceiling heights vary, screens separate drinking areas and different levels create a modern feel to this evidently historic building. Live music of the '*easy listening*' style provides a diversion from the norm, starting oddly at four in the afternoon. Sing-along-a-bus-stop maybe? Those buses will be handy for the trek along the Rochdale Road. I would certainly put this pub on my route to the ground. The beers will rotate from the W+D list, they are already changing regularly. The pub deserves its rebirth as a real ale outlet, the town needs it and hopefully they will support it for many years to come.

BWV 27.4.06: Mansfield *Cask Bitter*, Smiles *April Fuel*

SUBSCRIBE NOW

to Britain's Longest Running Football Fanzine

available now from

PO Box 56, Bradford BD13 3XW

or email Mike at *miketallgent@btinternet.com*

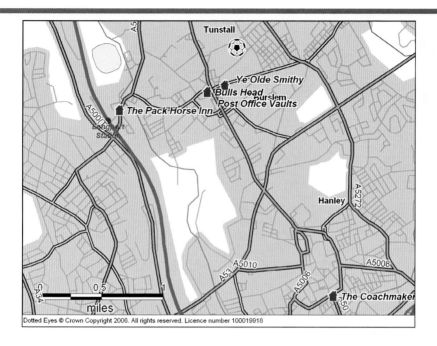

Dotted Eyes © Crown Copyright 2006. All rights reserved. Licence number 100019918

Bulls Head

14 St. John's Square, ST6 3AJ. Telephone 01782 834153
Gaffer: Bob Crumpton
Food: Bar snacks only from 12
Smoking Throughout
Open: 3 to 11 Mon to Thu, 12 to 11 Fri to Sun.

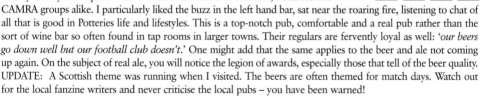

Lovers of Titanic ales will make an extra effort to find their brewery tap in the main town square, within a mile of the Vale. This is by far the best pub at this end of the Potteries and the locals will rightly tell you just how great it is. It has a fairly clubby atmosphere and is indeed the home of climbers, ramblers and CAMRA groups alike. I particularly liked the buzz in the left hand bar, sat near the roaring fire, listening to chat of all that is good in Potteries life and lifestyles. This is a top-notch pub, comfortable and a real pub rather than the sort of wine bar so often found in tap rooms in larger towns. Their regulars are fervently loyal as well: *'our beers go down well but our football club doesn't.'* One might add that the same applies to the beer and ale not coming up again. On the subject of real ale, you will notice the legion of awards, especially those that tell of the beer quality. UPDATE: A Scottish theme was running when I visited. The beers are often themed for match days. Watch out for the local fanzine writers and never criticise the local pubs – you have been warned!

BWV 10.3.05: Titanic *Anchor, Best, Black Ice, White Star,* Vale *Special*
BWV 2.12.05: Belhaven *St. Andrews Ale,* Cairngorm *Trade Winds,* Titanic *Anchor, Best, Iceberg, Legend, Oilslick, White Star,* Thatcher's *Cheddar Valley Cider*

The Coachmakers Arms

65 Litchfield Street, Hanley, ST1 3EA. Telephone 01782 262158 **New**
Gaffers: Jason Barlow and Sue Grocott
Smoking Throughout
Open: 12 to 11.30, 12 to 12 Fri and Sat, 7 to 10.30 Sun

Andy McCormack of a Vale fanzine came up trumps with this offering. Having tramped the streets for two days, with some very mixed success, the final call was something of a reward. The Coachmakers is run by Jason and Sue and immediately I entered I felt I had found a new home. The humour of landlord and locals was instant, and the choice of ales, refreshingly interesting. They may only have been there a few years but the pub offers something out of the ordinary.

The oddities include a preservation order on the shelf in the corridor bar! Another is the cool (or is that cold?) outside toilet. It has notices on the ceiling to question your sobriety, and a landlord who, by his own admission, '*knows more about nuclear physics than footie.*' Weird! The pub itself deserves some description. It has four rooms and that corridor, the largest of which is unbelievably the home of Sunday jazz sessions once a month. Each has beautiful tiles, fires, and/or timber walls. No room is large enough to accommodate a large group of lads. I shared a really pleasant afternoon pint or two with Trevor, a CAMRA enthusiast. On matchdays both Stoke and Vale fans will use the pub. During the week the time will be spent in the company of the professional classes who quite happily travel distances to use it. Who could blame them?

BWV 2.12.05: Acorn *Sovereign*, Burton Bridge *Burton Porter*, *Stairway to Heaven*, Coach House *Gunpowder Mild*, Woodlands *Full Bodied Bitter*

The Old Smithy

50-52 Moorland Road, ST6 1DT. Telephone 01782 827039
Gaffer: Adam Keenan
Smoking Throughout
Open: 12 to 12, 12 to 1am weekends.

The pub is designated as very much a home-fans-only pub with the police directing fans to the nearby Vine. The evidence of my sources do suggest, however, that there are plenty of real ale fans who have found '*the place to be totally welcoming and non-threatening.*' If there was one piece of policing policy that needs to change, then that is it. My evening visit found the weekly quiz taking centre stage and European football was a minor distraction on the background screen. It has a separate pool room bar, a large lounge and upstairs function room. It has no pretensions of being anything other than a real pub. It also appeared to be a popular locals' haunt with plenty of good reports of quality ale on tap throughout the week. Very soon I was introduced to the local CAMRA crew who were meeting upstairs. Good choice folks and thanks for the info. As for the quiz, what was Britain's first tabloid newspaper? It will be very busy on Port Vale matchdays. *UPDATE:* The pub has been redecorated and the policy re away fans is a little more relaxed. They are also known to have groups book the upstairs function room, having called Adam in advance.

BWV 10.3.05: Everards *Tiger*, Greene King *IPA*, *Old Speckled Hen*, Wells *Bombardier*, Worthington *Cask Bitter*
BWV 2.12.05: Bass *Draught*, Greene King *Abbot*, Wells *Bombardier*, Worthington *Cask Bitter*

The Pack Horse Inn

Station Street, Longport, ST6 4NA. Telephone 01782 577322 **New**
Gaffer: Keith Ward
Food: A good steak pub with a full all-round menu.12 to 2, 6.30 to 9
No Smoking in restaurant
Open: 12 to 12

SP	TV	BM	D

This is the pub that the locals recommend for food and a pint, especially if you are in a family group. Keith, an Everton fan, is well known locally as a landlord who knows the tastes of his regulars. So the '*Landlord's choice*' may be a mystery but inevitably it is a good one that changes every few weeks. Sam behind the bar, is equally helpful, if a little confused, about his new allegiance to the Vale, having Leeds United roots.

    The pub is very much in the village-local style. Quite roomy, it is carefully divided by wrought iron screens into two sections. The restaurant specialises in steaks and becomes a drinking room when the nosh stops. In the summer the canal provides some extra passing trade. It is also the first pub one sees when taking the obvious route from the A50 into Burslem. A meal will be well walked-off by the 20 minute or so trek up the hill. Lazy old me would take the 98 bus from outside the pub door. The lunchtime trade draws from local workers; at the weekends the professional classes come out to play, using the neat courtyard on the hot summer days. Entertainment is of the pub-singer and karaoke style with quiz-nights thrown in. This all adds up to a great local that has something a little extra. And so it was that I left the pub to Sam still bleating about '*the goal that never was*' as a couple of Wolves fans came in to eat and chat about the beautiful game.

BWV 2.12.05: Coach House *Dick Turpin*, Courage *Directors*

Post Office Vaults

3 Market Street, Burslem, ST6 3AA. Telephone 01782 811027 **New**
Gaffer: Patrick Hayes
Smoking Throughout
Open: 11 to 11, 12 to 11 Sun

MP	SKY	BM

The Post Office stands out in the centre of a town where there are masses of pubs, many serving real ale but few having something different to standard national ales. It looks really attractive from the outside and is remarkably tiny when you go inside. The '*Postie*' should really be the '*postage stamp*': if thirty people could squeeze in, then I would be amazed. So it is then that this great little pub deserves your early custom. You will find a good welcome and beer that has both national standards but also an interesting guest.

    Pat, a Shrewsbury fan with Vale affections, was sporting a No. 37 Grumpy shirt when I called. Nothing could be more misleading. He knew everyone who entered by name and beer choice. It would be almost impossible to not get into conversation here. The footie enthusiasm was seen as Soccer AM was amusing the locals in a pre-midday warming-up pint session. When I talked to locals about the apparent liking for grim buildings as pubs they replied, quite rightly, '*that it is what is on the inside, which is beautiful.*' Aah. Bless! The Post Office is both beautiful inside and out and should be part of anyone's mini-crawl around town. The regulars are typically mixed in both age and sex. The consistency, as Pat has found in his short time in the pub, is that the real ale attracts "nice folk" to good locations. That was certainly the case here.

BWV 2.12.05: Fuller's *London Pride*, Greene King *Abbot*, *IPA*, Titanic *Night to Remember*

Port Vale

Burslem is the historical mother of the Potteries, if not a mother of a place. This club was founded in a house called Port Vale, although we can find no history of the house or the odd name. The ground is next to Burslem Park; which is a well maintained park in the Victorian style of a series of levels and intimate spaces. It is also the site of one of Vale's previous grounds.

Old Town Hall

People do not usually stare at buildings and chuckle, but this town centre building, described as a 'Corinthian temple perched on a railway bridge,' should bring at least a smile, even if it has been turned into a commercial site.

Burslem town has kept a basically mediaeval street plan, and has some Victorian buildings worth seeking out, including the wonderful *Wedgwood Institute* on Queens Street which has terracotta panels by Lockwood Kipling, father of Rudyard.

Rudyard Lake

This is a reservoir to the east of Burslem, near Leek, a technical and aesthetic triumph designed by John Rennie in the 18th Century to supply the Leek Canal. Rudyard Kipling was named after this lake, probably not for the reason that the Beckham's named Brooklyn; but because Lockward (obviously already used to odd names) proposed to Alice Macdonald here. Rudyard was born in India; his first language was Hindustani. His poems work brilliantly as spoken pieces as long as the audience is not half strangled with beastliness.

Rotherham

This town feels similar to a few others of middling sized that grew from a mix of early market centre and later industrial development. There is a large mediaeval church which is worth looking around if you have a spare 10 minutes or so.

The town has some small but pleasant museums. The Clifton Park Museum (Clifton Lane) is a town museum in the town centre, something many towns lack; Rotherham Art Gallery (Walker Place) is small, with ever changing exhibits; and the York and Lancaster Regimental Museum, in the same building, will appeal to small boys of all ages and genders, although it has more models and medals than guns, so some will leave disappointed. The most obvious mark of humanity is inhumanity. War is about hell, but it is also about sacrifice and glory, and museums like this serve to remind us of both sides.

Rotherham Market

This had a stall selling magazine back issues, so you could buy something to read during a match. It is worth looking to see just what people will produce a magazine about. We are sure that we will, one day, find a magazine called: 'Organ Grinders Monthly' which will be full of tuning tips and monkey care advice. We will then discover that it has at least two rivals: 'Organ!' Which will be full of colour photos, and: 'Grinder's Gazette' which will be full of black and white photos, and stories of organ grinding in the old days.

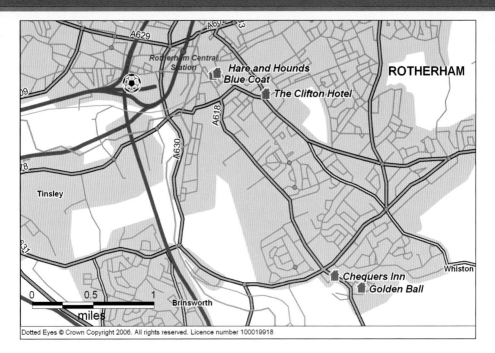

Dotted Eyes © Crown Copyright 2006. All rights reserved. Licence number 100019918

Blue Coat

The Crofts, Moorgate, S60 2DJ. Telephone 01799 539500
Gaffer: John Wall
Food: Traditional pub food from sandwiches to steaks plus curry nights 9 to 11
Separate smoking areas
Open: 9 to 12 Sun to Thu, 9 to 1 Fri and Sat

This is no ordinary version Wetherspoons but one with a well deserved reputation for good ale and quality knowledgeable service. The team are all CAMRA members and I am assured that the beer selection is innovative and constantly changing. When I visited all beers were on offer and the staff certainly impress with their enthusiasm for the trade. You know the design features, save to say it rambles over different levels and is a pub rescued from a nightclub existence. I will be back to this one, perhaps drinking in the planned beer garden or maybe listening to live music, well that would certainly be different.

UPDATE: This is the local CAMRA Pub of the year for 2006. Jazz has arrived on Monday nights, sometimes with John on Trombone. Four beers rotated while I visited over a lunch time such is the popularity of the beer selections. Watch out for the specialist beer festivals (fruit in August etc.) The improvement has also spread to the Rhino, the alternative 'spoons in town.

BWV 15.3.05: Acorn *SPA*, Caledonian *Deuchars IPA*, Eastwood *Gold Award*, Kelham Island *Pale Rider*, Marston's *Burton Bitter*, *Pedigree*, Wentworth *WPA*, *Bete Noire*, Weston's *Old Rosie*
BWV 9.5.06: Acorn *POTY Time*, *Sovereign*, Banks's *Chocolate Mild*, Bullmastiff *Son of a Bitch*, Caledonian *Dr. Bob's Magic Potion*, Everards *Original*, Marston's *Pedigree*, Titanic *Lifeboat*

CP | TV | BM | PG | D

Chequers Inn

Pleasley Road, Whiston S60 4HB. Telephone 01709 829168
Gaffers: Tony and Ann Manderson
Food: '*Good food served as fast as we can*', all freshly sourced, home-cooked and very good value. 12 to 2, 4.30 to 7 Mon to Fri, 12 to 3 Sun
Separate smoking areas
Open: 12 to 11 Sun to Thu, 12 to 11.30 Fri and Sat

There were numerous recommendations that I should put this pub in the guide. I have no hesitation in doing so for it is indeed, a really good pub that has a good reputation for its very friendly, welcoming atmosphere. The Chequers is a large tavern, set back from the road and attractively redesigned to mix the modern, open-plan style with traditional beer and food values. It was voted local CAMRA pub of the season for Spring 2006 no doubt in part due to the policy of regularly rotating the ales around TT Landlord. I made my two visits returning because I liked the place so much. It offers both space for large groups and intimacy when groups congregate in the tap room for a football match on the TV or to play darts. It also has a pool area, raised above the general level.

The food certainly made an impression on me. The regulars come from long distances to the Chequers. At the risk of being a beer estate agent, the village of Whiston is a high value location, three great pubs and a really pleasant semi-rural environment. Tony has created a good real ale house in his short time here. It is how the suburban family orientated beer and food pub should be, having good quality and ample choice in both beer and nosh. It isn't a typical football pub but it is well worth a pre-match pint.

BWV 9.5.06: Bateman *XXXB*, Timothy Taylor *Landlord*, Tetley's *Cask Bitter*, *Dark Mild*, Wells *Bombardier*

SP | TV | JB | PG | D

The Clifton Hotel

105 Old Clifton Road, S65 2AW. Telephone 01709 833070
Gaffers: Joanne and Mark Kelly
Smoking Throughout
Open: 4 to 11.30 Mon to Thu, 12 to 12 Fri and Sat, 12 to 11.30 Sun

Rotherham's real ale scene has improved dramatically in the last year or so, due in no small part to landlords such as Joanne and '*Arnie*' who are introducing local drinkers to a wider range of ales. John at the Blue Coat pointed the way up the hill to the Earth Stadium, opposite which you will find the Clifton.

It is a grand old street-corner hotel with quite a history if you believe the regulars. You know when you have found something special when a chat with the landlady soon develops into a really pleasant group discussion with the locals who draw new arrivals in to the chat to add their two pennyworth. Jo introduced '*24 year old*' Billy who in turn brought in Dave and soon the stories of the pubs' past came out. Tales of a town gaol house with gallows for the sinners on the rugby field over the road merged with recollections of a more recent gentlemen only room. The ex MP lauded the pub recently, no doubt he agreed with its award of CAMRA Pub of the season for spring 2006. The pub is obviously very busy when the Titans play. It is a good twenty minute down hill walk to the ground but conveniently this will take in the other town recommendations en route. On other days it will be music and then general knowledge quizzes to entertain, plus the social club style check night on a Sunday. This gives the biggest clue as to how this is a proper locals pub where the pub becomes the centre of the community in which it is placed. One can only predict that the future is bright for this boozer.

BWV 9.5.06: Greene King *Old Speckled Hen*, Stones *Bitter*, Wadworth *6X*

Golden Ball

7 Turners Lane, Whiston S60 4HY. Telephone 01799 726910
Gaffer: Joanne Bird
Food: Extensive menu to suit all tastes from traditional to international 12 to 9
Separate smoking areas
Open: 12 to 11 Sun to Wed, 12 to 12 Thu to Sat

Continuing my rather unusual entry for Rotherham I followed the advice of all I met in town, and travelled out to this pretty village near to the M1. There are three ale houses in the village but it was the Golden Ball that caught my eye. This is a typical Ember Inns refurbished pub, but the quality of the ale is what makes it memorable. The pub has a high '*Your Mother in Law would like it factor*' but there were plenty of variety in the lunchtime eating crowd. This is a real pub, with plenty of space for the restaurant style trade. I would recommend a trip here, combine it with lunch and even consider catching the bus into town (The No 34, every 15 minutes, plus others from opposite the Chequers).
UPDATE: Joanne is the new boss and the pub appears even busier than last year. I chatted with Heather outside over a great beer about the possibilities for a repaint in the next year. It was very much a business lunch session. The pub now holds popular real ale festivals.

BWV 15.3.05: Adnams *Broadside*, Greene King *IPA,* Shepherd Neame *Spitfire*, Stones *Bitter*, Tetley's *Cask Bitter,* Timothy Taylor *Landlord*
BWV 8.5.06: Bass *Draught*, Caledonian *Deuchars IPA*, Timothy Taylor *Landlord*, Tetley's *Cask Bitter*

Hare and Hounds

52 Wellgate, S60 2LR. Telephone 01799 821554
Gaffer: Carol Mills
Food: Home cooked, traditional pub food 11.30 to 2 Mon to Fri
Smoking Throughout
Open: 11.30 to 11, 11.30 to 10.30 Sun

The Hare and Hounds is a rescued pub. Closed and derelict in the recent past, it is now building a reputation as the rare Rotherham feature, a real ale pub. It was a very pleasant visit, the spirit of warmth and friendship coming instantly to the fore. The pub is very much a community pub with regulars who form very different groups at different times of the day. My lunchtime visit found the football highlights being shown on Sky TV while others were chatting or reading papers over a quiet lunchtime pint. The pub does get quite busy and the beer garden acts as overspill on summer days. I didn't meet the landlord that day as he had organised a trip for locals to the Bateman brewery, top geezer. Greene King ales come as norm, supplemented by national guest ales carefully selected to meet the locals taste. This is the best non-chain option in town; if only the demand from the locals was such that others could experience the delights that the variety of real ale could offer.
UPDATE: The pub was equally friendly when I visited again this year. It is totally unchanged and a popular locals' recommendation.

BWV 15.3.05: Adnams *Broadside*, Greene King *Abbot*, Weston's *Cider*
BWV 9.5.06: Adnams *Explorer*, Greene King *Abbot*

FOOTBALL AND REAL ALE GUIDE

PREMIERSHIP PUB OF THE YEAR
As voted for by the readers 2006-07

The Anvil
Dorning St, Wigan

BWV 1.3.05: Hydes *Anvil*, *Dark Mild*. Merlin *Cannonball*, Phoenix *Arizona*, Rooster's *Yankee*

BWV 5.6.06: Hydes *Bitter*, *Mild*, Phoenix *Arizona*, Rooster's *Yankee*

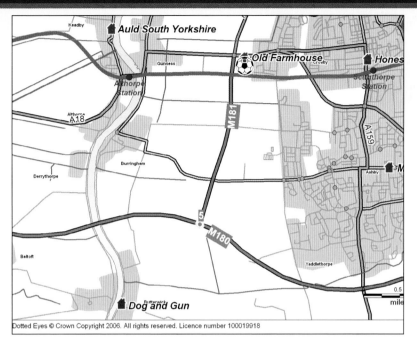

Dotted Eyes © Crown Copyright 2006. All rights reserved. Licence number 100019918

Auld South Yorkshire

Trentside, Keadby, DN17 3EF. Telephone: 01724 783518 **New**
Gaffer: Kevin Doughty
Food: All home-cooked menu including steak and ale pie and fish dishes
12 to 2, 6 to 9 Mon to Fri 12 to 9 Sat, 12 to 6 Sun
Separate smoking areas
Open: 3 to 11 Mon to Thu, 12 to 11 Fri to Sun

| CP | TV | JB | PG | D |

I am glad that I can include this attractive, award-winning local to the choice in the guide. Kevin runs a true village pub, down to local football sides as well as darts sides. It is the food that attracts many couples to the pub and it is certainly obvious that it is popular. In my brief lunchtime visit there were several bookings being taken for birthday parties, champagne and all.

A pool table occupies the smaller bar to the right while the larger, carpeted lounge is the preferred location for ale and food samplers. To the rear is an almost separate area that would be perfect for those CAMRA meetings, regularly held here. Kevin has a football fan pedigree, being in a past life the driving force of the Leeds United Supporters Club. As you would imagine, he is used to welcoming away fans who have found this pub over the years. Those wanting a bit of industrial heritage could do worse than take a walk along the adjacent canal and wonder at the functions of the Trent in British geographical history. Walkers and barge-dwellers use the pub and its garden in summer. For myself, the apple pie proved very tempting but I declined it in favour of a rare chance to sample the regular Daleside ale. The other beers change after each barrel, usually from popular brands. Despite the signs outside, this is a genuine freehouse.

BWV 27.1.06: Daleside *Best Bitter*, Theakston's *Best*

Dog and Gun

High Street, East Butterwick, DN17 3AJ. Telephone 01724 782324
www.darktribe.co.uk
Gaffer: David (Dixie) Dean
Smoking Throughout
Open: 6 to 11 Mon to Wed, 5 to 11 Thu and Fri, 12 to 11 Sat and Sun

New

CP · TV · BM · PG · MP

I just know that you will go the extra mile to find something very special. The Dog and Gun is well out of walking distance and so its delights are limited to those who can organise a driver to take you there. The pub is very much a work in progress. Dixie has moved the nationally-renowned DarkTribe brewery from Gunness to the rear of this 200 year old river side inn. He is working with great gusto to create what makes the proper traditional pub. It has roaring log fires in winter, tiled floor in the bar, and; something unique in my experience, the return of the Dog and Gun bus seats. So much for trendy café bars, this pub can be compared to a buffet bar as found in a bus station. Further developments include the re-opening of the room that once had a pool table, and the enclosure of the outside loos. This development may not be so popular with the local postman who shared this convenience with me before opening time.

The regulars travel from the many surrounding hamlets, desperate to find a real pub, while the locals devote their efforts to food and lager. In summer this is perfect cycling country and, being so remote, makes a good destination point for walkers on the levee that lies opposite the pub. A Saturday visit will find Judy at the helm. On Sundays the pubs' team might be sampling a post-match ale. I really look forward to revisiting this next year as no doubt the pub establishes a fine reputation as the DarkTribe tap.

BWV 27.1.06: DarkTribe *Full Ahead*, *Old Gaffer*, John Smith's *Cask Bitter*

Honest Lawyer

70 Oswald Road, DN15 7PG. Telephone 01744 849906
Gaffer: Allan Edgar
Food: Restaurant upstairs specialises in quality home cooked food
12 to 2, 6.30 to 9
Smoking Throughout
Open: 11 to 11 Sun to Thu, 11 to 12 Fri and Sat

B

SP · SKY · BM · D

This is by far my favourite pub in Scunthorpe for real ale; it has style in everything it does and it comes highly recommended from fans across the country. The Honest Lawyer is a small, long bar with wooden floors and panelled walls. This busy pub has it all: quality, knowledgeable service, good conversation and regulars who love footie and real ale. My recent second visit found the company of Scunthorpe fans who were all too ready to help out with the essential taxis to the ground for our group of travelling real ale and footie fans. We were then able to watch the lunchtime game and sample from six real ales without any real worry of missing the game.
UPDATE: Timothy Taylor and Daleside ales now form the staples in the real ale diet that now has six or more real ales. Match-day specials are also on the menu.

BWV 16.10.04: Archers *Harvest Ale*, Gale's *Trafalgar*, McConnell's *Irish Stout*, Wychwood *Hobgoblin*, Young's *Special*
BWV 27.1.06: Butcombe *Brunel*, Caledonian *Auld Lang Syne*, Daleside *Bitter*, Exmoor *Hart*, Greene King *Ruddles County*, Isle of Arran *Fireside*, Timothy Taylor *Landlord*, Wild's *Wild Night*

Malt Shovel

219 Ashby High Street, DN16 2JP. Telephone 01724 843312
Gaffer: Michael Pogson
Food: Good value home prepared food, specialising in fish choices
12 to 2, 4 to 7 Mon to Thu, 12 to 2, 3 to 7 Fri and Sat, 12 to 7 Sun
Separate smoking areas
Open: 10 to 11, 12 to 11 Sun.

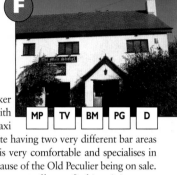

| MP | TV | BM | PG | D |

Set back from the suburban village Ashby High Street and attached to a snooker club, this is a pub that asks questions. How does it balance restaurant trade with great beer choice? Why can't other Scunny pubs offer this? How much is a taxi to the ground? It is large enough for the restaurant and ale fans to be separate having two very different bar areas but I would use this pub if I wanted good food with quality ale. The pub is very comfortable and specialises in traditional English food as well as ale. The locals tell me it is very popular because of the Old Peculier being on sale. They also enthuse at the relaxed attitude to real ale tickers who have made an extra effort to find it as it is not on the usual town centre or station routes. So for me it is a pub to find early in the day, grab a meal, sit in the seat with a view through the leaded windows and decide if it is a taxi or buses to the ground.
UPDATE: The pub is totally unchanged.

BWV 16.10.04: Abbeydale *Moonshine*, Bateman *XXXB*, Courage *Directors*, John Smith's *Cask*, Salamander *Eddy*, Theakston's *Old Peculier*
BWV 27.1.06: Abbeydale, *Moonshine*, Courage *Directors*, Skinner's *Jingle Knocker*, Tom Wood *Dark Mild*, John Smith's *Cask Bitter*, Theakston's *Old Peculier*, Wild's *Wild Night*, Wold Top *Mars Magic*

Old Farmhouse

Glandford Park, DN15 8TE. Telephone 01724 276376
Gaffer: Brian Henderson
Food: Traditional varied menu to suit all tastes, with midweek offers
11 to 10 Mon to Sat, 11 to 9.30 Sun
Separate smoking areas
Open: 11 to 11 Mon to Sat, 11 to 10.30 Sun.

| CP | TV | BM | D |

The Old Farmhouse is a large Tom Cobleigh restaurant/bar in the typical style of modern examples. It is well organised and, whilst it gets busy on matchdays, there is always room. Watching a summer game is best as everyone spills out into the garden. It has a no-colours ban but it doesn't take long to convince the landlord that you are not a problem and then to find out that Brian is a real footie expert, knowing many people within the game. '*It is rare to find a pub in a new ground complex that is a real pub*'. So ignore your reservations about modern pubs and give it a go. Yes it includes a Wacky Warehouse and is geared during the week to families eating out of town. Yes it is large and typically modern in design. Yet it is a very friendly place that is always staffed for bigger crowds and I have yet to go in and not be welcomed as an away fan. Also every visit has included sampling good guest ale, put on for weekends during the season.
UPDATE: There are plans to reinstate real ale using cooling jackets. This was lost to visitors in the last season.

BWV 16.10.04: John Smith's *Cask Bitter*, Tetley's *Cask Bitter*
BWV 27.1.06: *NO REAL ALE*

Scunthorpe

The five little villages that make up Scunthorpe grew like a rash after 1835 to process the iron ore the town was built over and on, but they were not united until 1935! This may explain why Scunthorpe still does not feel like a town, but does not explain why, with five names to choose from, it was called Scunthorpe: especially as the parish church was at Fordingham.

Scunthorpe is isolated, so local shops can prosper by selling to local people but, with no cinema and with North Sea winds keeping folk indoors, the town feels very inward looking. On the other hand the heavy industry here used to result in spectacular sunsets, but not spectacular enough to keep your mind off the Arctic chill.

The Corus Steel Works

This is a spectacular sight. It makes railway rails and much more, and provides 4000 jobs; the sort of jobs that give self respect to workers and prosperity to a town, something retail parks and call centres never can. These jobs mean Scunthorpe does not have to fret over its image. Corus run open days but only in summer. They are also host to the *Appleby-Fordingham Railway Society*, who run their own steam hauled tours on the plant's rail network. *www.afrps.co.uk.*

Scunthorpe has a lot of green open space. There are also museums, but they are not listed on the web under Scunthorpe, but under North Lincolnshire, which is daft.
www.northlincs.gov.uk/NorthLincs/Leisure/museums

Swansea

Swansea Bay

It is a simply stunning sweep of seascape, although you have to cross the frighteningly busy "A" road and walk along the front a little to fully appreciate it.

Swansea's Museums

All the museums are within the Harbour redevelopment. Swansea Museum is a traditional town museum, and all the better for it. The *Transport Museum* is very small, and it may have been eaten by a bigger predator museum, but worth a look if it has survived.

Dylan Thomas Museum

The display here is well thought out and works for fans and for people who are just curious. There is also an excellent book shop.
www.swansea.gov.uk/index.cfm?articleid=1044

Swansea Evening Post

An excellent paper. The C.E.O of Bradwan was born in Gorseinon just to the west of Swansea. On his last visit this was enough for him to be featured in the paper!

Castle

It is a large lump of rock that most folk just walk past, but it is worth pausing for a look. The toilets nearby are also a must see. They are simply the cleanest and best looking loos we have ever used. How can Swansea manage this when free public toilets in England are becoming rarer than competence within the FA?

Market

Swansea is still famous for shellfish and this is the place to try it. Laverbread is also available. If you like spinach you will love this seaweed.

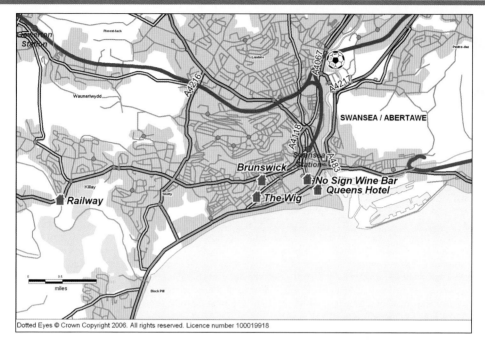

Dotted Eyes © Crown Copyright 2006. All rights reserved. Licence number 100019918

Brunswick

3 Duke Street, SA1 4HS Telephone 01792 465676
www.thebrunswick.mysite.wanadoo.co.uk
Gaffer: Allan Rohman
Food: Home-made food with daily specials 12 to 2.30, 6 to 8
Smoking Throughout
Open: 11.30 to 11.30

Beer from the barrel? Yep. The ale picks from the S+N list works here. It was so good I visited Allan's pub three times over two days and every time there was a different guest on offer. My match day visit was one that confirmed my view that the good people of Swansea match any town for friendliness allied with appropriate footie fervour. The pub itself is in a farmhouse style, with a simple long bar, barrels behind one end. The room is subdivided by wooden screens that allow quite large groups to congregate in corners to talk about the meaning of life and football. Allan is the perfect host and well worth seeking out to get the low down on other pubs in town, the ones that are a treat and the ones to give a miss. His creation here stands up well by comparison.

UPDATE: Allan is still here and the Brunswick is going from strength to strength. One innovation is the art work on the walls. On my visit the work of Bruce Risdon was particularly diverting. As a Swansea fringe venue the pub it has a town-wide importance. It is also now an acoustic music venue.

BWV 5.11.04: St Austell *Tribune*, Brains *Bread of Heaven*, *SA*, Courage *Best*, Young's *Special*
BWV 25.11.05: Brains *Bread of Heaven*, Courage *Best*, Fuller's *ESB*, Greene King *Ridley's Old Bob*

MP · TV · BM · D

No Sign Wine Bar

56 Wind Street, SA1 1EG. Telephone 01792 465300 **New**

Gaffer: Philippa Shipley

Food: All home cooked, freshly prepared menu with signature dishes 12 to 10, 12 to 5, 6 to 9 Sun

Separate smoking areas

Open: 11 to 11 Mon to Wed, 11 to 12 Thu to Sat, 12 to 10.30 Sun

Cocktails and wine in a football and real ale Guide I hear you ask. Well this is Swansea and Wind (Wine) Street is the new trendy version of Kingsway and will no doubt be where the masses gravitate on match days as there is no, I repeat no real ale out near the inaptly named Liberty Stadium.

The bar is 85 metres long and has been extended far into the rear in traditional wine bar style i.e. wooden vaults and hanging vines. The clientele is also mixed with couples and families filling the front bar along with what appeared a very determined hen party starting a full day of celebrating. The No Sign has a heritage that has references in Dylan Thomas's Followers as the Wine Vaults in Paradise Alley. The more obvious history is as the Vaults of Mundays Wine Vaults and this name is taken in the subterranean music venue that adds to their eclectic appeal. The manager talked with enthusiasm that no two days are the same as the pub has a few regulars but many returning customers who having discovered its virtues return because it is the best town centre location for good ale, wine and freshly cooked food. The ale was in top order and the atmosphere perfect for a lone beer hunter who relished the chance to sit and take stock of the beer scene in Swansea. The attempt to introduce guest ales is proving popular and no doubt the No Sign will be on the real ale map for some time.

BWV 25.11.05: Brains *SA* Greene King *Ridley's Old Bob*, Ruddles *County*, Palmer *Copper Ale*

SP · SKY · JB · PG · D

Queens Hotel

Gloucester Place, SA1 1TY. Telephone 01792 521531

Gaffer: Gary Owen

Food: Completely traditional Welsh cuisine 11.30 to 2.30

Smoking Throughout

Open: 11 to 11, 12 to 11 Sun

This marina pub has a justifiable proud landlord. Set among converted warehouses with picture windows the high ceilings and massive mirrors ooze a touch of class without any pretensions of grandeur. The Queens Hotel proved to be a popular matchday pub, several discrete away groups came and went without masses of interaction, getting a good hearty meal and then being left to enjoy the pub as a good friend would. The pub is a rare Welsh outlet for Theakston's, very popular apparently with the locals. Have you seen the bear? You can't miss it, standing bouncer like near the door. I have used the pub on many occasions especially combining it with the tourist bits that are now found along the once desolate town dockside. Not far from the town centre it will now be a taxi ride to the new stadium. Because it is out of Kingsway and away from the big town pubs, it avoids the hassles sometimes found when so called local English teams visit the self-appointed Welsh capital. *UPDATE* 25.11.05: Guest ales now change more regularly and include local brews. Sea shanty festivals also centre on the Queens Hotel.

BWV 5.11.04: Buckley's *Best*, Theakston's *Best*, *Mild*
BWV 25.11.05: Buckley's *Best*, Theakston's *Best*, *Old Peculier*, Tomos Watkin *Merlin*

Railway

553 Gower Road, Upper Killay, SA2 7DS. Telephone 01792 203946
Gaffers: Rory Gowland and Adrian Martin
Smoking Throughout
Open: 12 to 2, 4 to 11, 12 to 11 Sat, 12 to 10.30 Sun

This is your archetypal country cottage pub. Having small rooms off a tiny bar
the theme is on village life and long gone railways. One of only two Swansea
brewery pub outlets this is as good as it gets in the Swansea area. The regulars
know their beer and will readily share that enthusiasm. *'It is a good place for
those who like to cycle and drink.'* (On a converted rail track cycle way) My visit
coincided with an evening petanque match, all very sociable, leaving room in the bars for the serious ale heads. In
fact my taxi ride to the pub proved money well spent as the choice of ales kept changing and another undiscovered
beauty came into view (I'm talking about the beer, ok). Unfortunately the pub is not convenient to the railway line
despite its name so you will need to convince a non-drinking driving friend to get you to the match. A top pub in
a great location!
UPDATE: CAMRA regional pub of the Year 2005. The pub has changed not a jot and the beer choice is still
fantastic.

BWV 5.11.04: Jennings *Redbreast*, Shepherd Neame *Spitfire*, Swansea *Original Bitter*, Three Cliffs *Gold*,
Bishopswood, Deep Slake *Dark*
BWV 25.11.05: Archers *Ghost Train*, Robinson's *Unicorn*, Swansea *Bishopswood Bitter*, Deep Slake *Dark*, The
Original *Bitter*

The Wig

134 St. Helens Road, SA1 4BL. Telephone 01792 466519 **New**
www.thewigswansea.co.uk
Gaffer: Rob Dawson
**Food: Good value for money menu including Welsh specials and themed
nights. 11.30 to 8. Sun 12 to 4 carvery, 12 to 8 in the bar**
Separate smoking areas
Open: 11.30 to 11 Mon to Thu, 11.30 to 12 Fri, 12 to 12 Sat, 12 to 11 Sun

The Wig was recommended by the regulars at the Brunswick as the best of the
other Uplands pubs. Rob and Lynda's welcome is such that instantly one feels
that you have found a pub that is improving rapidly and will be a good real ale house for years to come. Rob tailors
the ale to his locals' tastes to include lighter beers on big match days.

It was interesting to see how, on my visit, the regulars gravitated towards the large picture windows where there
is a view out over the patio.. The mix of patrons was very mixed, ranging from students cuddling a beer for an hour
to regular lunch takers eating no doubt on expenses before a return to the nearby offices. The reputation for real
ales is gained by 20 ales being available in a typical week, changing regularly and offering something new with each
visit. So it was that I sat in one of the window seats, none of Joe's ice cream was seen and Breconshire ales sampled
for this drinkers' first time. I could imagine long hot summer evening spent on that patio, on winter evenings
perhaps the corners of the bar would be more welcoming. At any time the Wig is an example of how a modern
refurbishment can be done without losing the local nature of a community pub.

BWV 25.11.05: Badger *Tanglefoot*, Butcombe *Gold*, Breconshire *Red Dragon*, Greene King *Old Speckled Hen*,
Tomos Watkin *OSB*

FOOTBALL AND REAL ALE GUIDE

CHAMPIONSHIP PUB OF THE YEAR

As voted for by the readers 2006-07

Bridge Bier Huis

2 Bank Parade, Burnley

BWV 17.12.04: 3 Rivers *IPA*, Archers *Seasonal Greetings*,
Bowland *Baa Humbug*, Hydes *Bitter*, Saxon *Midnight Hour Cider*

BWV: 12.06.06: Cottage *Germany Calling*, Everards *Svengal Tiger*,
Hydes *Original*, Milestone *Black Pear*l, Three B's *Bee on the Ball*

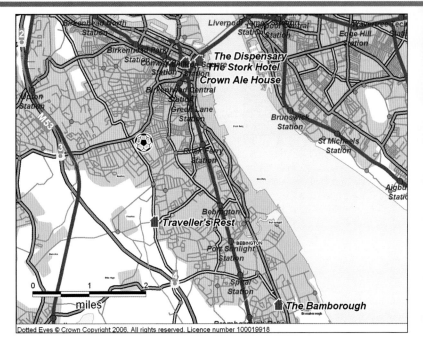

The Bamborough

2 Bamborough Village Road, Bamborough CH62 7ES. Telephone 0151 3342113
Gaffer: Geoff Naylor
F Good value, traditional and '*giant*' pub food 12 to 9
Separate smoking areas
Open: 11 to 11 Mon to Thu, 11 to 12 Fri and Sat, 12 to 11 Sun

| CP | SKY | JB | PG | D |

Suburban Wirral has many large estate pubs that are popular with Football fans. Given that many come via the southern motorway link I travelled to one such '*village*' that has a choice of these pubs and found the best it had was the Bamborough. Unlike some of its near neighbours there is an instant welcome and care for the stranger who visits. Quick service and a friendly smile set the tone and the choice of ale that changes regularly met with my familiar home palate

This pub is a classic sports pub of the Sky sports variety. Decorated in the modern style and with large screens it would be perfect for the pre match premiership offering. It is easy to imagine that it will be packed on those long Sunday afternoon sessions that can seemingly last all day when the fancy takes. On other days the lunchtime clientele consists of family meal groups, often elderly fathers footing the bill. By the evening the locals come in for regular sessions, they could have a private section each if they so wished. Most will gravitate to the more traditional front bar for locals chat and banter. It is a very friendly place, somewhere that could easily become a home from home. Not in the cosy back-street way but in the style of the ever more common Greene King estate mode. My advice is to use this if you and your friends are driving to the game and want easy food choices and a leisurely drive on to the ground. Don't expect a real ale fest, do expect some space to sit and relax.

BWV 18.4.06: Greene King *Abbot*

CP SKY JB PG D

Crown Ale House

128 Conway Street, Birkenhead CH41 6JE. Telephone 0151 6502035
Gaffer: Anne-Marie Canavan
Food: Home made Irish stew all day
Smoking Throughout
Open: 11 to 11 Mon to Sat, 12 to 10.30 Sun

This pub is an imposing sight from outside and equally impressive within. As one enters, the highly polished beautiful rooms off an ornate central bar make an immediate impression. My choice was to sit in the leather clad bar benches and marvel at the Cheapside mirror tiling while dreaming of the next beer. Three visits in a year suggest that I really like this pub. Kevin, the former licensee has moved on but the reputation of the pub continues and extends well beyond the Wirall. Get there early on matchdays as it will be busy. On other days the pub is home to TV supporters and the pubs own teams. As Mike of Birkenhead says *'Tranmere Rovers fans meet here pre and post game and have a good rapport with genuine away supporters, many returning regularly.'* So I will be back one day soon, (If only it was to watch my Rovers!) It is a top pub, no doubt.
UPDATE: The exterior was been repainted and a new roof installed as I visited. All part of the improvements made since Anne-Marie arrived. The beer choice is still as impressive.

BWV 28.2.05: Evan Evans *Cwrw Welsh Ale*, Titanic *Captain Smith's*, Cains *Bitter*, John Smith's *Cask*, Theakston's *Mild*, York *Stonewall*
BWV 18.4.06: Cains *Bitter*, *Dark Mild*, Courage *Directors*, Greene King *Ruddles County*, John Smith's *Cask Bitter*, Shepherd Neame *Spitfire*, Timothy Taylor *Landlord*, Worthington *Cask Bitter*

MP TV BM

The Dispensary

20 Chester Street, Birkenhead CH41 5DQ. Telephone 07709 814126
Gaffer: Mary Ruhe
Food: Traditional home-cooked menu, locally sourced and with fantastic Sunday lunches 12 to 7 Mon to Sat, 1 to 5 Sun
Smoking Throughout
Open: 11 to 11, 12 to 7 Sun

Mary and Tony returned to the 'Dizzy' in March 2005 and have embarked on a regeneration of this classic Victorian bar that will surely make it something that is truly special. It already has character by the shed load. The high ceilings and unique roof windows are interesting in their own way, so too is the way that the pubs steps into the rear on three different levels, each spotless and gleaming in their different light.
It is a family run pub, all muck in to create a friendly fun pub that serves the full range of Cains' ales and seasonal guests. The food is very popular, especially the legendary Sunday roasts that are both well-priced and locally sourced. The humour is orchestrated by Tony. *'Why don't you ever hear father in Law jokes'* was the thought for the day. The *'Dizzy blondes'* make the events tick, but neither are truly blond nor dizzy, but the party atmosphere is apparently mad if the photos are any form of evidence. There are plans to open up the function room upstairs; presently it is a home to the pool fraternity. My lonely preference would be to take advantage of the free papers and sit on the newly arriving bench seats, pausing to reflect on local gossip and engage in banter with friendly footie fans from both sides of the watery divide. As you probably guess I really liked the warmth of this long and narrow bar.

BWV 18.4.06: Cains *2008 Celebration Ale, Bitter, FA, IPA, Triple Hop*

The Stork Hotel

41 Price Street, Birkenhead CH41 6JN. Telephone 0151 6477506
Gaffer: Karen Murphy
Food: Good quality wholesome pub food 12 to 2, 4.45 to 6.30 Mon to Sat,
2 to 6 Sun
Separate smoking areas
Open: 11.30 to 11 Mon to Sat, 11.30 to 10.30 Sun

| SP | SKY | JB | PG | D |

The Stork Hotel is a pub that throws up surprises of the best variety in every visit.
It is a really big real ale pub in a grand building that has true architectural merit. The
four ales are ever-changing, so quickly that I record here only those on at lunchtime,
the evening menu is likely to be totally different, such is the turnover. Enthusiasm for top notch ale pours out of the
William Morris wallpaper. The warmth and humour shouts out from the many corners of this multi-roomed gem.
Much of the fun comes from the staff and their keenness to promote traditional ales from independent breweries.
Revered as the best pub that Birkenhead has to offer, the locals come from all over the Wirral using the metro that
arrives nearby. Beer trips were being planned with the regulars; the beer sounded great but camping in Snowdonia
would evoke too many childhood nightmares for this pampered poodle. Dave orchestrates the beer selections to a
tee. He will also gladly tell you of the remarkable discoveries made as the pub has been restored to its glorious past.
The removing of a carpet unearthed majestic tiled floors, the opening of spaces discovered the news room that is
now so smoke-free you can positively smell the past. There are four equally splendid rooms; the old boys
congregate in the front tap room, the luncheon-taking office workers retire to the high-ceilinged lounges off to the
rear. Add in a great garden for a barbeque or ale festival, and what you find is a great real ale pub.

BWV 18.4.06: Archers *Wet Dream*, Copper Dragon *Bitter*, Everards *Tiger*, Holt *Fifth Sense*

Traveller's Rest

169 Mount Road, Higher Bebington CH63 8PJ. Telephone 0151 6082988
Gaffer: Ann Irving
Food: Wonderful home-cooked menu 12 to 2 No food Sun
Separate smoking areas
Open: 12 to 11 Sun to Thu, 12 to 12 Fri and Sat

| SP | SKY | D |

This highly recommended street-corner *'village'* local is very convenient for
those arriving via the M53. Timber-framed lounges make up the bars around the
central bar, all brass and country kitchen style. It has a loyal set of locals who
relish it being a proper pub. They enjoy a range of national favourites
supplemented by regional guests. My visit found family groups and town office workers enjoying the good pub
food. Beware if you prefer baseball caps or shell suits, the Governess will not make you as welcome as her real ale
crew. Quite right, although in a pub I owned, I might in one of my more fantastic moments, add in Blackthorn
insignia or anything red (There goes half my sales then) Ann was very helpful, particularly in pointing me in the
right direction to town centre pubs. I would certainly return. Oh for the days of Friday nights watching Tranmere
away
UPDATE: Nothing has changed but the friendliness gets even better.

BWV 28.2.05 Flowers *IPA*, Timothy Taylor *Landlord*, Boddingtons *Cask*, Greene King *Abbot, IPA*, Weetwood
Oathouse Gold
BWV 18.4.06: Flowers *IPA*, Greene King *Abbot*, Goose Eye *Bitter*, Jennings *Cumberland Ale*, Shepherd Neame
Spitfire, Timothy Taylor *Landlord*, Wells *Bombardier*

Tranmere

The Wirral is a odd place. Parts are as flat as Norfolk, and parts feel like the Stone Age has not yet began. Birkenhead grew with steam ferry services from Liverpool in the 1820's. In 1827 William Laird created a shipyard and had massive plans for Birkenhead, and Hamilton Square is a grand result: but the plans failed, and that seemingly twisted the face of the town forever: but things seem to be improving.

New Brighton

It had a tower to rival Blackpool, yet in August 1991 it had been utterly forgotten; the tourist office had shut for its holidays, there wasn't a B&B to be found, and the beach had, apparently, been washed away when the new Liverpool container dock changed the Mersey's flow.

The Lady Lever Gallery

Built by William Hesketh Lever (of Sunlight Soap) as the centrepiece of his town of Port Sunlight, and opened in 1922 to display his amazing collection which began with a pottery shepherd and shepherdess he bought for his mantelpiece. We would recommend this place whole heartedly if it was not full of confusing sings about coats and bags: and if we had not been confronted by an attendant, hours after entering, with: 'The museum has a policy. You put your coat on, or you put it in the cloakroom.' With neither a "Please", Nor an 'Excuse me!' The Lady Lever may be an easy drive from Liverpool in a twocked car, but there are better ways of scally screening than this.

Yeovil

The Beach

This is what the locals call a big lawn which is 20 miles from the sea. It is below the church of St John, which is worth a look if you like churches.

Yeovil's museum, now rebranded as The Museum of South Somerset, seems to have been tarted up in a sympathetic way. The building used to be the Coach House of Hendford Manor.
www.southsomersetmuseums.org.uk

Fleet Air Arm Museum

If you like war planes this is a 'must see'. The Fleet Air Arm was the Royal Navy's air force, and it is worth learning something of how it had to fight the Battle of the Atlantic to stop Britain starving. It did so with battered old biplanes because there was no money left after the RAF were bought thousands of super expensive modern bombers: bombers which in the first three years of the war missed their targets by an average of 20 miles and caused more casualties to RAF Bomber Command than to Germany! The museum is to the north of Yeovil and there is an entrance fee.
www.fleetairarm.com

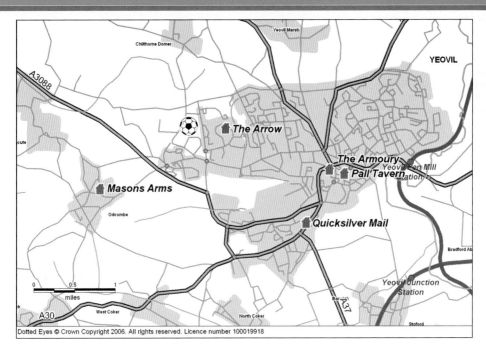

Dotted Eyes © Crown Copyright 2006. All rights reserved. Licence number 100019918

The Armoury

New

1 The Park, BA20 1DY. Telephone 01935 971047
Gaffer: Martin Kotecki
Food: Good value pub menu
12 to 2.30, 5.30 to 7.45 Mon to Sat, 12 to 2.30 Sun
Smoking Throughout
Open: 12 to 12

The Armoury and football and real ale legend dates from Conference days; the ties lasting because fans of fellow promoted teams continue to make their journeys via the pub.

SP	SKY	JB	PG	D

    Martin has maintained a reputation for real ale based on Wadworth ales, a regular Butcombe guest and a range of rotating beers. The pub is very much sports-orientated having two big screens for TV games and areas set aside for both pool, table football, bar skittles and darts. The pub also has a skittle alley that occasionally doubles as a function/overspill room when it is very busy. This will happen when the locals gather for the evening. During the day there is a mix of shoppers finding a quieter place outside the town centre for their lunch, and local office workers meeting over a pint or two. I preferred the back bar where there are big country kitchen tables, perfect for groups to meet and join in the pub banter. The atmosphere is jovial in the style of the friendly landlord and bar staff. Mel certainly made this stranger feel instantly welcome. The Armoury is large enough for both Yeovil and visiting fans to mix. This will be a friendly pub to do so, as so often reported by fans who suggested that I visit. My suggestion is that the Armoury is the obvious last stopping off point for those wanting a crawl in town, before getting a taxi to the ground.

BWV 28.5.06: Butcombe *Bitter*, St. Austell *Tribute*, Wadworth *6X*, *Henry's IPA*

CP · SKY · BM · PG · D

The Arrow

The Forum, Stourton Way, BA21 37L. Telephone 01935 476972 **New**

Gaffers: Kevin Mahon and Jacky Barnes

**Food: Good value innovative menu with special football menu on match days
12 to 9**

Separate smoking areas

Open: 2 to 11 Mon to Sat, 12 to 10.30 Sun

Any visit to the South Coast should involve drinking Ringwood ales and here on a pleasant estate can be found an Eldridge Pope tavern that serves ever changing options from that brewer. The Arrow is also a mere five minute walk from the new Huish Park, in the middle of a housing estate that would normally send me walking in the opposite direction when beer-hunting. It was a brilliant surprise to find that the Arrow is so much more than the typical big estate chain pub.

Kevin and Jacky arrived in April 2006 and have created both a proper local and a family-orientated community pub. This is due in part to the sheer size of the place. One end is devoted to food while the other is subdivided by screens and tables to create small areas for small group drinking. One little idiosyncrasy is the arrangement of football club mugs; in league order that change with the football results. Another brilliant design feature is the raised stage area with big screen that is subject to change as the TV layout is altered to meet the demands for watching big screen events. The pub is very sports friendly. Families coming to those long Sunday afternoon sessions will find that there is also a large patio and garden for outside drinking. During the day the office workers arrive from Westlands, the Fleet Air Arm and Screwfix. The evening clientele reflects the professional make up of the local estate.

BWV 28.5.06: Ringwood *Best, Fortyniner*

Masons Arms

41 Lower Odcombe, BA22 8TX. Telephone 01935 862591

Gaffers: Paula Tennyson and Drew Read

**Food: Top quality home cooked menu, both bar and a la carte sourced from
named local sources 12 to 2, 6.30 to 9.30**

Separate smoking areas

Open: 12 to 2.30, 6 to 12

CP · BM · D

F

This is a beautiful thatched local, all geared up to meet the needs of those who want good ale in a picture-postcard village street. Add in a brewery on site and the recipe is there for a good lunchtime session. Paula and Drew moved in just a few weeks after my last visit and the improvements are just remarkable. The home based brewery now provides 36 gallons a week of great ale exclusively to the pub The bar and restaurant are always busy with food customers and locals drinking. They are joined by an increasing number of tourists finding their way to this '*off the beaten track*' pub, where the atmosphere is pleasantly bubbly at all times.

The pub also offers en-suite accommodation and a certified campsite with views across the valley towards Yeovil. Gentle, quiet, traditionally furbished with a peaceful beer garden for sunny days, the pub deserves your custom, it won't disappoint. I would also consider using this pub to break up a journey further South-West, combining a weekend away with a walk in the classic Somerset landscape found in the nearby hills or coastline. The micro-brewery ales were a refreshing surprise that set me up well for the ritual humiliation of the Yeovil Town thrashing later in the afternoon,

BWV 10.2.05: Otter *Bitter*, Wells *Bombardier*, Taunton *Cider*

Pall Tavern

Silver Street, BA20 1HW. Telephone 01935 476521
Gaffers: Geoff and Moyra Harrington
Food: Good value pub menu 12 to 2.45, 6 to 9 No food Sun eve
Smoking Throughout
Open: 11 to 11

MP	TV	BM	PG	D

The Pall name comes from Coffin Cloth. Well this pub was dead and gone a few years ago. The resurrection is in full swing and Geoff and Moira are creating a traditional town pub that serves good real ale without the usual trendy paraphernalia; rather a full size pool table and good conversation is enough for my tastes. They do accommodation as well; phone to make a great weekend on the way out west. I'm not sure about the local's tipple of Blackcurrant and Vimto though. For me it was excellent Port Stout and plenty of time chatting to Geoff about the pubs past and more refreshing future. Yeovil town centre isn't overly blessed with real ale pubs, some other good pubs are also reluctant to welcome away fans but that is not the case here, it's the real ale that does it. So after walking up from the distant station, should the police allow you to do so, then the Pall Tavern makes a good first port of call. Even better, make it a pint on your way home.
UPDATE: The pub has a snooker room upstairs. The Pall Tavern is basically the same and is now the only local CAMRA GBG entry in town.

BWV 10.2.05: Greene King *Old Speckled Hen*, Ruddles *County*, O'Hanlon's *Port Stout*
BWV 28.5.06: Greene King *Old Speckled Hen*, Ruddles *County*, Ringwood *Boondoggle*

Quicksilver Mail

108 Handford Hill, BA20 2RG. Telephone 01935 424721
Gaffer: Pete Lambden
Food: Good variety of hot and cold meals Breakfast from 8am
11 to 2.30, 6 to 9, 11 to 3 Sun
S Separate areas
Open: 11 to 12, 11 to 11.30 Sun

CP	TV	BM	PG	D

The popularity of this pub lies in its appeal to all ages and tastes. One day the regulars were lunching couples and real ale hunters like me. The following matchday saw the famous old footie fans coming out for a reminiscence of glories past and now present. The pub has genuine links with professional football, just tease it out of Pete and a chat about the good old days is guaranteed. It is a good refurbished pub keeping features like the large darts/function room that is the home of the Ciderspace team. The company is really friendly and has the advantage for road travellers of having a car park and being both well away from the town centre and ground. The guest beers always include some regional specialties, unnamed here but they are there. This would be food pub choice; it certainly proved popular on my visit It is the best that Yeovil can offer and footie friendly; just perfect.
UPDATE: The pub offers good value accommodation; the number of rooms has increased in the last year. Pete has Cask Marque accreditation. The pub remains as popular as ever and increasingly so among away fans who love good ale,

BWV 10. 2.05: Adnams *Broadside*, Butcombe *Bitter*
BWV 28.5.06: Adnams *Broadside*, Butcombe *Bitter*, Otter *Bitter*

FOOTBALL AND REAL ALE GUIDE

DIVISION TWO PUB OF THE YEAR

As voted for by the readers 2006-07

Birkbeck Tavern

45 Langthorne Road, Leytonstone

BWV 25.1.05: Barnsley *Oakwell Bitter*, Rita's *Special* (*House Brew*),
St. Austell *Tinners*, Skinner's *Betty Stogs*

BWV 12.4.06: Archers *Spring Blonde*, Rita's *Special* (*House Brew*),
Welton's *Old Cocky*, *Randy Rabbit*

Join CAMRA today and receive a free ticket to the 2007 Great British Beer Festival, Earls Court

Over the last thirty five years, CAMRA, the Campaign for Real Ale, has been campaigning on all different kinds of beer and pub issues. We have helped to save breweries and pubs, helped to introduce more flexible licensing hours and run numerous beer festivals but our work doesn't end there!

CAMRA now boasts over 82,000 members and we are striving to reach 100,000 members to help us with our future campaigns.

By becoming a CAMRA member you can help to make a difference.

CAMRA membership represents great value. For just £18 a year, that is less that 35p a week. If you join our organisation you will also benefit from the following:

- A monthly copy of our colour newspaper 'What's Brewing' – this includes news on the pub and brewery industry, information on what is happening in your area, lists of CAMRA beer festivals around Britain, features on different real ale breweries plus much more!
- Free or reduced entry to over 150 CAMRA beer festivals, including the Great British Beer Festival
- Discounts on CAMRA books including our best selling Good Beer Guide
- The opportunity to become an active member of the organisation – All members are welcome to attend branch meetings, socials, sign petitions to save pubs and breweries that are under threat from closure and survey pubs and bars etc. CAMRA membership means different things to different people.
- Complimentary Clubs – these clubs are exclusive to CAMRA members and are free to join. Clubs currently running include Fuller's, Hook Norton, Everards and Woodforde's. Complimentary Clubs offer members a variety of promotions including free pint vouchers, brewery trips, competitions and merchandise offers. Please visit *www.camra.org.uk/joinus* to find out more.

CAMRA Membership makes the perfect birthday gift!

Do you have a friend or family member's birthday coming up? If so, then CAMRA membership offers something completely different to the usual socks you buy Dad or flowers you buy Mum! If your friend or family member enjoys their beer and pubs then a year's CAMRA membership is the ideal present. Your present will consist of the benefits already mentioned earlier in this article and can be delivered to your address or direct to your friend or family member.

Join **CAMRA** today and receive a free ticket to the 2007 Great British Beer Festival, Earls Court

CAMRA's recent highlights

- CAMRA was instrumental in lobbying for new flexible licensing reforms in England and Wales which allows pubs to apply for extended licenses that appeal to the local community.
- Our annual Parliamentary reception in Westminster gave us the opportunity to lobby over 100 MPs, Lords and researchers.
- CAMRA awarded their Pub Design Awards in January 2006 which gives recognition for innovative and imaginative design. CAMRA is now judging pubs that will be awarded in January 2007
- CAMRA announced their National Pub of the Year in February 2006. The award went to The Swan, Little Totham, Essex. This is the second time they have won this award!
- National Pubs Week, which encourages pubs to organise and promote events throughout the week to help reduce pub closures, was the most successful generic pub campaigns so far. Over 10,000 pubs participated in February 2005
- CAMRA has set up a Complimentary Clubs initiative which allows CAMRA members to sign up for free and receive a variety of exclusive benefits including free pint vouchers, brewery tours, competitions etc. There are currently four of these clubs – Woodforde's, Fuller's, Hook Norton and Everards. Please visit www.camra.org.uk/joinus to read more.
- Manchester hosted a successful sell-out National Winter Ales Festival
- CAMRA presented the first Cider and Perry Pub of the Year award to The Miners Arms, Lydney, Gloucester
- CAMRA has launched a number of books including the Good Beer Guide 2006, London Pub Walks, Good Pub Food, Cider Guide, Big Book of Beer and the Good Beer Guide Germany.
- CAMRA has organised over 150 beer festival around Britain

Join CAMRA today, quote '*Football Real Ale Guide*', and receive a free ticket to the 2007 Great British Beer Festival

CAMRA is offering everybody that joins CAMRA through this Football and Real Ale Guide a free 2007 Great British Beer Festival ticket. All you need to do is visit *www.camra.org.uk/joinus* or call 01727 867201 and quote '*Football Real Ale Guide*' as your promotional code.